EVANGELICALISM IN BRITAIN 1935–1995

EVANGELICALISM IN BRITAIN 1935–1995

a personal sketch

OLIVER BARCLAY

INTER-VARSITY PRESS

Inter-Varsity Press
38 De Montfort Street, Leicester LE1 7GP, England

© Oliver R. Barclay 1997

First published 1997

British Library Cataloguing in Publication Data
A catalogue record for this book is available from the British Library.

ISBN 0–85111–189–0

Set in Garamond

Typeset in Great Britain by Parker Typesetting Service, Leicester

Printed and bound in Great Britain by The Guernsey Press Co. Ltd, Guernsey,
Channel Islands

*Inter-Varsity Press is the book-publishing division of the Universities and Colleges
Christian Fellowship (formerly the Inter-Varsity Fellowship), a student movement linking
Christian Unions in universities and colleges throughout the United Kingdom and the
Republic of Ireland, and a member movement of the International Fellowship of Evangelical
Students. For information about local and national activities write to UCCF,
38 De Montfort Street, Leicester LE1 7GP.*

CONTENTS

PREFACE

The 1935–95 period was one of dramatic changes in the evangelical scene. Those who are looking for a full history of the evangelical movement over the years since 1935 must be aware that this is not my aim. This book covers neither the whole church in Britain nor the developments among evangelicals outside Britain. It is a study of *trends* in British evangelicalism that seem to be important and have a bearing on our situation today. It is inevitably something of a personal sketch, written from my own exposure to people and literature during this period. It is not therefore an academic 'historian's book', though it is concerned with the story of these years. Professional historians may find little of significance that is new to them, apart from the value of the personal experience of one who lived through this exciting period. Rather, I have tried to trace the key changes over this time, as I see them, and some of the causes of those changes. Since there are plenty of people alive today who can be consulted for each phase of this period, I have drawn on first-hand impressions from a good number of them, either by letter or by direct contact.

When I started as a student in 1938 – the year of Munich – I already knew several of the leaders of both conservative and liberal evangelicalism, some leaders of the Church Missionary Society (CMS) and the Student Christian Movement (SCM), and some members of the Oxford Group. Nearly all of these were known to me through family connections (my father was Far East Secretary of the CMS). Some of them urged me to join the university's Christian Union, and others pressed me to join the SCM and not to get caught up in something so small as the CU.

Since I have known more of the leaders of evangelical Anglicanism than those of other churches and have been closely involved in student work ever since 1939, this study may seem to be too biased in those directions. I believe, however, that what happened in those circles was typical of what was happening more widely in less clear ways. My personal perspective can therefore illustrate main trends even if it is not exhaustive.

Presumably we ought to try to learn from history. The Bible, after all, contains a great deal of history 'for our instruction' (1 Cor. 10:11). I am not, however, a professional historian, and write rather as someone who is trying to detect any theological or spiritual changes (which are usually neglected by academic historians) and to see if there are principles that we can learn from them. Professional historians usually concentrate on cultural and social influences, and those things have been fully dealt with by others. I am much indebted to their writings for a great deal of factual information, particularly David Bebbington, Randle Manwaring, Adrian Hastings and B. G. Worrall, whose works I shall refer to later. Ian Randall, T. A. Noble and the late John Wenham allowed me to see some very useful unpublished material. Others have been generous in correspondence. I have had constructive comments from a number of people who have read all or some of the book in draft, but I do not name them here in case they are held responsible for the whole of the book. I shall refer to them in the notes where particularly relevant. I must, however, name my wife, Daisy. She not only provided me with constructive criticisms and corrections, but also encouraged me as I went along and accepted my absorption in the task when she had reason to hope that I would be more free for other things.

Leicester   *Oliver Barclay*
April 1997

1. WHO IS AN EVANGELICAL?

In the late 1920s, Hensley Henson, the then Bishop of Durham, famously described evangelicals as 'an army of illiterates, generalled by octogenarians'. He was not altogether alone in such an opinion. In the 1990s the situation is clearly very different. Evangelicals are generally accepted as an important factor in the life of the churches, and evangelical churches are full of educated young people. Why were they so scathingly dismissed in the 1920s and 1930s, and why is their situation so different today? Such a resurgence of lively evangelical life is seen by evangelicals themselves as due to the unusual blessing of God and not primarily to human agencies. It is important, however, to ask what we can learn from the weaknesses of the 1930s and from the developments that have transformed that situation so markedly.

What is evangelicalism?

First, it is essential to have some sort of definition of evangelicalism, or at least an outline of its essential character. The movement has always had its varieties of emphasis, and has inevitably sometimes been dominated by one or two issues of the day or by its leading personalities. A long-term view has advantages, and can identify the core elements, which are often referred to today as 'classical evangelicalism'.

John Stott has often been quoted as describing evangelicals as both 'Bible Christians' and 'gospel Christians'.[1] That is a good description but does not distinguish them from others sufficiently for many purposes. Writing in 1983 he expressed it like this: 'I want to argue that the evangelical faith is nothing other than the historic Christian faith. The evangelical faith is not a peculiar or esoteric version of the Christian faith – it *is* the Christian faith. It is not a recent innovation. The evangelical faith is original, biblical, apostolic Christianity.'[2]

Stott is right to say that evangelicals have always reaffirmed the great Reformation emphases of justification by grace alone, through faith alone and by Christ alone because, like the Reformers, they found them in the Bible. These truths are part of any orthodox Protestant faith, but do not always distinguish evangelicals from other Protestants. The Reformation stress on 'Scripture alone' (discussed below) had ceased to be generally accepted outside evangelical circles by the twentieth century, even by many who professed to hold to the other 'alones'. This was therefore one major distinguishing mark of evangelicals throughout our period. In an age in which almost anything can claim to be a Christian view, evangelicals stand out as having certain clearly identifiable features, even while they claim to be in the mainstream of orthodox biblical faith.

Taking a broad sweep from the 1730s to the 1980s, the historian David Bebbington defines evangelicalism in terms of four *distinctives*: conversionism, activism, biblicism and crucicentrism.[3] Although they provide an outline for a long view, I believe they should be put in a better order and they need to be more exactly defined for our purposes in the twentieth century. Bebbington's outline has the advantage that it emphasizes three doctrinal features, and without this doctrinal framework evangelicalism dissolves into a vague set of attitudes. The evangelical position is necessarily circumscribed by doctrine because, as the New Testament shows, doctrine determines everything else – or should do so. Alister McGrath, writing in 1996, defines evangelicals in essentially the same four terms. They undoubtedly provide a useful outline.[4]

What Bebbington calls *biblicism* – a term of abuse in some circles – needs to be defined in terms of seeking above all else to be ruled in life and thought by whatever is the teaching of Scripture. Because evangelicals accept it as the Word of God written, all other authorities have to give way to it. This is the Reformation doctrine of the final authority and sufficiency of the Bible. There is a massive difference between those who respect the Bible as one source of revelation equal to others, and evangelicals, who have accepted the Bible's own emphasis on it as uniquely authoritative (as for example in 2 Timothy 3:16–17). By the 1930s, evangelicals were effectively the only section of the British churches that held to this truth. This implies a doctrine of biblical reliability that was implicit, but not necessarily always explicit, in those who simply trusted and obeyed whatever they found in the Bible. It has been the claim of evangelicals that, like the Reformers, they are 'Bible Christians' – seeking to follow the Bible in all matters of faith and conduct – and this controls the other doctrinal and ethical positions.

Crucicentrism also has to be further defined for our purposes. As Bebbington himself puts it, 'the standard view of evangelicals was that Christ died as a substitute for sinful mankind'.[5] In the period that we are considering, it was also a clear criterion of the difference between evangelicals and liberals and often between evangelicals and the high-church party. Ever since the Reformation, this emphasis on substitutionary atonement has been a characteristic of evangelicals. It has enabled them to explain how it is that salvation must be *by Christ alone* (others could set an example; no-one else could possibly atone for sin) and *by grace alone through faith alone* (Christ has done all that is needed; to try to add to it is an insult). Without a belief in substitutionary atonement, it is also almost impossible to lead people to a proper assurance. Assurance of salvation entirely on the basis that Christ 'bore our sins in his body on the tree' (1 Pet. 2:24) is another usual, but not quite universal, feature of evangelicalism.

Bebbington's word *conversionism* needs to be defined in terms of the need for people to experience a real spiritual change – to be born again by a work of the Holy Spirit. This stress on the need for a personal experience of God through new birth does not depend on any particular kind of conversion. That 'lives need to be changed', as Bebbington describes the idea, is often held by others in a way that evangelicals would not recognize as the same thing as biblical conversion.

Activism will be discussed later, but at the start of this period it majored on evangelistic activity almost to the exclusion of social activity, except local philanthropy, as far as the UK was concerned. In any case, it is more a typical practical outcome of the faith in the God of *revelation, redemption* and *regeneration* defined in the other three features. Activism is important, however, because those who are theologically at one with evangelicals but do not have a vision for evangelism (if there are such people) can hardly be called evangelicals in any modern sense. Thus, in popular parlance, being an evangelical is often confused with being evangelistically minded. Evangelicalism and evangelism should go together, but are not the same thing.

What I think is chiefly missing in Bebbington's description is something so fundamental that it is easy to take it for granted – though it must never be taken so. That is, the essentially *Christ-centred* nature of the evangelical position. The cross can become a cold doctrine, the Bible a mere collection of precepts, and the new birth a merely psychological experience, if they all do not depend totally on a personal relationship with the living Jesus Christ himself. This has been the mark of most evangelical renewals, often in subtle rather than explicit ways. John Wesley summed up his message when he said, 'I offered Christ to them.' The contrast between evangelicals and a rather dead orthodoxy has often been expressed in this focus.[6] The apostle Paul says that he determined to preach to the Corinthians 'nothing . . . except Jesus Christ and him crucified' (1 Cor. 2:2), and this determination has moulded evangelical ministry ever since. Sometimes, it must be admitted, this has entailed the relative neglect of the doctrine of God the Father – as was often true in the 1930s.

Conservative, classical, liberal

These five features describe what in the 1990s tends to be called *classical evangelicalism* (CE). That is a useful title because it recognizes that the mainstream of evangelical religion over centuries has had these marks. At the start of our period, however, the term in use was 'conservative evangelical' to distinguish it from those who described themselves as 'liberal evangelical' (LE). For the purposes of this book I shall refer to 'classical' or (to use the older term) 'conservative evangelicals' by the abbreviation 'CE', meaning those who maintain a doctrine of the reliability, sufficiency and final authority of the Bible, and as a result maintain also the substitutionary character of the atonement and seek to bring people to an experience of new birth. I shall use the term 'liberal evangelical' (LE) for those who, while they maintain some of the other typical evangelical emphases, do not maintain, and often repudiate, the total reliability of the Bible and usually do not preach substitutionary atonement, even if they stress the cross in a doctrinally undefined way. They also usually speak of 'deciding for Christ' rather than emphasizing the new birth.

The LE positions therefore shade off into frank liberalism where people would not wish to be called evangelicals. Alister McGrath characterizes liberalism as: 'insistence that Christian doctrines should be restated or redefined so as to render them harmonious with the spirit of the age'.[7] As such it is clearly a position that is unstable and subject to any pressures of contemporary culture – usually 'whatever seems reasonable' in the current climate of thought, reducing theology effectively to a branch of human philosophy. The LE position, as this period of history shows, shared in that instability. While the CE position can claim a very long history, the LE position is a relative novelty and its weaknesses have surfaced clearly only in this century.

The CE position as described above has to be distinguished from *fundamentalism*, although its detractors frequently try to charge CEs with all the extremes of American fundamentalism, as they did, for instance, when Billy Graham came to Britain in the 1950s. Fundamentalism has a different history, a very different ethos, and some important differences of substance, from British evangelicalism. Others have explored the differences recently, because they have found it still necessary to distance themselves from it.[8] Suffice it to say here that if, in the 1930s, British evangelicalism shared more of the emphases of American fundamentalism than would be true today, it soon shed the features that are usually in the minds of critics (as the following history shows). They share an honourable insistence on some of the key doctrines, but British evangelicalism was always more doctrinally mature and a less fierce reaction to others. As a result, it could grow into something that is today quite distinct and able to confront the culture in a much more positive way that avoids the charge of obscurantism.

By 1930 there was a clear division between the CE and LE traditions, especially in the Anglican and some Free Churches. The term 'liberal evangelical' was also in use in the Church of Scotland[9] in the 1920s and 1930s. The split of the Bible Churchmen's Missionary Society from the Church Missionary Society in 1922 had exposed the issues. A distinct and organized Anglican LE movement was created in 1923 as the Anglican Evangelical Group Movement (AEGM). They were glad of the title 'liberal evangelical'. In the student world the creation of the Inter-Varsity Conferences from 1919 and, in 1928, of the Inter-Varsity Fellowship of Evangelical Unions (IVF, now the UCCF)[10] as a formal movement, distinct from the increasingly liberal Student Christian Movement (SCM),[11] identified the key doctrines in its eight-point Doctrinal Basis.[12] These things distanced CEs from many who still regarded themselves as evangelicals but held a less robust doctrine of the Bible. That had led the LEs progressively into divergences on other doctrines. In the 1930s there were, of course, still a good many individual CEs in the LE movements such as the SCM. But as we shall see, the LEs tended gradually to be merged into the mainstream of the denominations, becoming indistinguishable as a movement, while its members became ever less clearly evangelical.

The backbone of evangelicalism was the CEs, who sought to maintain the basic Reformational doctrines, especially in the debates over the reliability and final authority of the Bible and the substitutionary nature of the atonement. English and Welsh evangelicals frequently defined themselves over against the high-church tradition, which was powerful in the university theology faculties and in the Anglican churches generally. That tradition, however, was usually 'orthodox' in the sense that it accepted the creeds, including the virgin birth, the bodily resurrection of Christ, and trinitarian beliefs. I shall refer to those who hold this tradition as 'orthodox' even when they are not evangelicals in the sense described above.

There was a fountain of basic evangelical doctrine, life and devotion that flowed not only from a strong belief in the reliability of the Bible but from the constant reading of it and expounding of it as the Word of God in the CE churches. LEs were often distinguished from CEs not so much by what they denied as by what they left out of their ministry. For example, when Psalm 95 (the *Venite*) was sung every Sunday morning, it became customary with Anglican LEs to stop at verse 7 so as to avoid speaking of the wrath of God and judgment. The omission of all mention of hell from Sunday schools had been officially recommended by the Methodist Conference before 1920.

The differences between CE and LE positions have frequently emerged in ethical issues as the decades have passed. At the start of our period, however, there was almost unanimity on ethical issues not only among all who described themselves as evangelicals, but also across a very wide spectrum including the high-church and even most explicitly liberal leaders. Many liberals were liable at that time to ask: 'Since we all believe in the Sermon on the Mount, what does it matter what else we believe?' Time has shown that it matters a very great deal.

I see no value in telling people who think of themselves as evangelicals that they are not 'true evangelicals'. I believe that it is better to ask whether they are CE, and to point out some of the long-term consequences in this period of abandoning a confidence in the Bible as the final and reliable authority in all matters of faith and conduct. I believe that it is important to ask what we can learn from this period of history. In particular, we need to ask whether it is possible to maintain and to revitalize the characteristic evangelical emphases if we do not have a strong diet of biblical teaching and preaching based on a robust doctrine of the reliability of the Bible.

2. PREWAR DOLDRUMS

The outlook for evangelical Christianity in the late 1930s was not very encouraging, even to most sympathetic observers. The great evangelical strengths of the nineteenth century seemed to have faded away, leaving only a remnant. It was remarked that evangelicals seemed to be losing rather than gaining ground, with their young people defecting to other traditions or losing faith altogether. People were being converted, but perhaps they were fewer than those who were being lost. There were occasional encouraging signs, but it needed faith to see them.

In the middle of the nineteenth century it had seemed that evangelicals might dominate the churches. It was said of them then, as it sometimes is today, that they had the ball at their feet. But just when they seemed to be strong and confident, perhaps too confident, decline had set in. Two main reasons have been given. I remember one historian expressing it like this in a lecture I attended while a student at Cambridge: 'Their first-class brains died in the swamps of West Africa, and they left theological education to anyone else who liked to take it on.' Secondly, he said, evangelicals had become rather legalistic and defensive against the increasingly powerful high-church party, getting involved in very public lawsuits against Romanizing tendencies. This tendency to spend too much time on attacking others gave them a largely negative image. Such criticism may have been necessary, but it was allowed to obscure more positive aspects of their witness. As a result they had also lost their place in the councils of the churches.[1]

The relatively small, conservative Presbyterian denominations in Scotland and Ireland had been forced on to the defensive. In the main Presbyterian

churches, although there were some individual, strong, conservative congregations, evangelical ministers were quickly absorbed into the presbyteries and
did little to help one another. The Free Churches in England and Wales were
in the same position, with no clear conservative groupings. Many who were
carrying on a good work in their locality became discouraged about having any
influence in the councils of their churches or gaining any other congregations
for a biblical faith.

There remained a distinct evangelical party in the Church of England, with
its own colleges, journals and conferences, but these were themselves
increasingly dominated by liberalism, and by the 1930s had ceased to speak
with a clear voice. Most of the staff at the colleges such as Ridley Hall,
Cambridge, and Rawdon College, Leeds (Baptist), were firmly LE. The
Anglican churches in Scotland and Wales were solidly high church, and many
of the evangelicals in the uniformly low-church Church of Ireland were LE,
leaving the CEs as a minority which has been described by one historian as
'tending to be inward looking, adopting a pietistic attitude; the clergy
concentrating on their parishes with little interest in the diocese or the wider
church'.[2]

It is worth surveying various aspects of this situation as a background to the
developments that followed.

The theological scene

In academic circles it was almost universally assumed that a CE view of the
Bible was dead. Those who held to it were regarded as theological dinosaurs on
their way to extinction. Even the relatively orthodox high-church party had
given way to the fashionable trends in biblical criticism, holding on to their
views because of tradition and not because they were clearly biblical. A liberal
view of the Bible held sway unchallenged in the theological faculties and in
almost all the literature that was appearing.[3] Many church leaders who had
been strong evangelicals in their youth were now unable to hold a conservative
view either of the Bible or of the atonement. Conservatives were usually
dismissed out of hand. John Wenham recorded that in 1935 his very
distinguished professor of theology, C. H. Dodd, had criticized a rather
conservative book more than once. He therefore called on him to ask just what
his criticisms were, only to be told that the professor had in fact never read the
book he criticized.[4] Hensley Henson's scathing description of evangelicals,
quoted earlier, was absurd in reality. Two of his chief targets were in their
sixties and were Cabinet Ministers,[5] but such a caricature was not unique.

Stephen Neill (an evangelical) wrote more objectively that 'evangelicalism was reduced to a level of less repute and less influence in the Anglican world than at any time in the preceding hundred and fifty years'.[6]

Liberal positions were then frequently more moderate than those that are common today. Many who had adopted a quite radical critical view of the Bible still claimed to believe the same old gospel truths that they had learnt from childhood, though certain aspects were less clear. Their more extreme views of the Bible now seem almost naïve. They found strong elements of animism in the Old Testament and adopted an evolutionary view of the path to monotheism. One much-used textbook, for instance, describes Jacob's experience at Bethel as 'the adaptation of an extremely local tradition which is made to apply to the God of Israel; but the remnants of animistic conceptions are as plain as anything could be'. That God appeared to Moses at the burning bush is dismissed thus: 'a more pointed illustration of animistic beliefs could not be given'.[7] Yet one of the authors (Theodore Robinson) claimed personally to believe and to pray as he had learnt at his mother's knee. What was difficult to cope with was the extraordinary confidence that this was the truth 'as plain as anything could be', and not pure speculation. The documentary hypothesis about the sources of the Pentateuch (J, E, D and P) was almost universally taught in ways that make it look silly today. As Ronald Knox expressed it, this 'reduced Moses to a syndicate of press-cutting agencies'.[8] It was then almost impossible to treat the Old Testament as in any meaningful sense the Word of God. New Testament criticism was also very sceptical about the words of Jesus and the authority of the apostles. G. T. Manley was heard to remark that theological professors followed one another like a flock of sheep, bowing to the authority of anyone who was a 'good scholar' in any field other than their own speciality.

The Free Church colleges followed the general trend, even the traditionally conservative colleges (apart from the Free Church of Scotland college). This was partly because in their anxiety to prove that they were as good as the university faculties they accepted anything that was described as 'the assured results of modern criticism'. The products of these colleges were frequently left to preach little more than some ethics. The Methodist colleges suffered as much as any, and of the Baptist colleges even Spurgeon's was considerably affected.[9] Apart from the London College of Divinity (now St John's College, Nottingham), the three other CE Anglican colleges (BCMS and Clifton in Bristol, and Oak Hill in London)[10] were very small and training almost entirely non-graduates. Their teaching was appropriate to that need. They

17

trained some fine practical ministers and missionaries, but they were not able to do theological battle. In Ireland, all Anglicans had to go through Trinity College, Dublin, and students of the Presbyterian Church of Ireland through Assembly's College, Belfast, which had no conservative teachers. In Scotland, the university faculties provided the only training for the Church of Scotland ministry, and they were overwhelmingly influenced by a liberal view of the Bible. In Wales, all theological training was in the hands of those who were liberal or very high-church, or both.

Conservative evangelicalism was a small faction in most denominations and had little influence outside its own circle. It is stated that only 3% of Anglican ordinands were evangelical. They felt they had their backs to the wall.

The theological establishment was so self-confident and aggressive that theological students who did not conform were frequently subjected to ridicule by fellow students and often by their tutors. If the newest first-year student did not have a quick reply to the lecturer's pronouncements, he was likely to be treated as incompetent. The doctrine of substitutionary atonement was scornfully described as the theology of the slaughterhouse. Theological students almost always came straight from school (especially in the Free Church colleges) or sometimes from an arts degree. In Ireland in particular, that meant that they were often only seventeen years old. It took exceptional strength to stand against the 'cultured despisers' of your faith, especially if you thought you were almost alone in doing so.

The result was that most of those who started their courses as apparently solidly evangelical finished up having lost their ability to preach the plain teaching of the Bible as the Word of God. Some became frankly liberals, but many simply lost their confidence and could only say, 'I believe . . .', with no greater authority than that. Some did recover their evangelicalism when they came to a crisis in their ministry and found that they had too little to say that was worth saying. They were driven to their knees before God. Ieuan Phillips in Wales, and Roland Lamb, were two prominent examples.[11] When they had studied theology they had concluded that they simply had not known the superior wisdom of the academics and decided that they had no choice but to give way to it. Ieuan Phillips used to relate how he was brought back to his evangelical roots when he found, at a friend's deathbed, that he had nothing to say. Few came out of their theological education totally unscathed. As a result, much evangelical leadership moved into the hands of lay people – doctors, scientists, schoolteachers and businessmen – who led the youth movements and provided a backbone for the missionary societies. The leaders who gave their names to the infant IVF as vice-presidents were nearly all scientists, medicals, soldiers and missionaries, with a few working ministers.

There were, of course, exceptions to this liberal consensus. T. C. Hammond in Ireland (though he left for Sydney in 1936), Professor Daniel Lamont in New College, Edinburgh,[12] and some of the Free Church of Scotland professors were respected scholars. (I always remember Lamont as an older man preaching for the CICCU – the Cambridge CU – and earnestly leaning over the pulpit to close by repeating his text: 'We pray you in Christ's stead, be ye reconciled to God' [2 Cor. 5:20, av]. Very few theological professors could have done that.) There were also individual lecturers in denominational theological colleges, though the universities tended to dismiss the college teachers as not truly academic. But individual teachers could not stop the overwhelming influence of the liberal tradition in theological education. The only textbooks available were in the liberal tradition. Evangelical students often survived by paying as little attention as possible to their courses, learning as best they could what they needed to equip them for the ministry, especially some New Testament Greek and church history. There were no recommended conservative theological books. Conservative students had to scour the secondhand bookshops for copies of Dale on *The Atonement*, Denney's *The Death of Christ* and commentaries by Lightfoot, Ryle, Ellicott, Handley Moule and others. No new conservative commentaries of any weight had appeared for a long time, and biblical studies such as the Keswick Bible readings were often rather loosely devotional with little careful exposition. Handley Moule was a favourite with some because he exemplified his own dictum: 'There should be no such thing as untheological devotion or undevotional theology.' He had been the first Principal of Ridley Hall, Cambridge, in 1881 and then became Professor of Divinity at Cambridge in 1899. In both capacities he had great influence in Cambridge through his teaching and writing, and in stabilizing the evangelicals in Cambridge when they were subject to extreme 'holiness teaching'. Sadly, since being made a bishop in 1901, he had more or less stopped writing and his books were out of print.

This lack of CE publications further strengthened the image of evangelicals as simplistic in their theology. One observer remarked ten years later that he thought there was only a handful of conservative evangelical vicars in the diocese of Gloucester, and that they were evangelical chiefly because they had read nothing much since they were in theological college thirty years before. Perhaps it was a help that the courses were so irrelevant to the task of preaching and pastoring that it was not thought a great loss to ignore much of the material! One future professor of theology said that he had to learn the relevant parts of theology almost from scratch once he got into the ministry. David Adeney, the future missionary statesman, called his course at Cambridge 'this miserable theology', and described it as specializing in 'undermining faith in the Bible as the Word of God'.[13]

The overwhelming influence was this self-confident liberal view of the Bible, which went with the conviction that only by this means could the gospel be made convincing to the modern age. The Second World War was to contribute considerably to the explosion of that myth, because a high proportion of those who came out of its horrors with any strong Christian convictions were people of a clear biblical faith, and the liberal optimism about human nature was made to seem very implausible.

The universities

Although the IVF was small and the university population was only 1.7% of the age group[14] (in the 1990s it is 32%), its growth was already significant. It provided a new kind of intellectually adequate classical evangelicalism and combined evangelistic zeal with doctrinal substance, while much of the CE community lacked one or the other. 1933 had seen the inception of what is now the Religious and Theological Studies Fellowship, and conferences for theological students were started in 1937. John Wenham played a prominent part in developing this work in 1937–39. As he expressed it: 'We could find no academically qualified theologian to help us. We students read papers to each other.'[15]

In the twenty-eight universities and university colleges, the Student Christian Movement, whose leadership was by now frankly liberal, was overwhelmingly stronger than the frequently very small Christian Unions that formed the IVF. Not all the universities and hardly any of the important teacher training colleges and technical colleges even had a CU. The IVF was also materially weak. In 1925–26, the Treasurer, Sylvia Berry (later Mrs Cecil Bewes), enjoyed saying that she kept the entire funds of what was to become the IVF in an Ovaltine tin in her bedroom! The Secretary of the Inter-Varsity conferences from 1925, and of the IVF from its formal constitution in 1928, was Douglas Johnson, always known as DJ. He did without his lunch sometimes in order to pay for the stamps on his numerous letters, written while he was still a medical student. He qualified only in 1930, after Professor Rendle Short (a surgeon and member of the Brethren) had persuaded him to leave London and give himself entirely to study for a year under the professor's eye in Bristol.

While the SCM had massive official support, the IVF was constantly under fire for its theological position and for being hostile to the rationalist traditions of a university. C. E. Raven, the Regius Professor of Divinity at Cambridge from 1932 to 1950, had written in 1928 that it was 'incredible' that anyone with the intelligence to pass Littlego (the very elementary university registration examination) should still believe in Jonah's whale and Baalam's ass.[16] It was sometimes said that the CEs were not in sympathy with the spirit of the universities and had no place there. If this meant that they were not rationalists,[17] then the charge had some substance, but it was not so long since theology had been called 'the queen of the sciences' and a revealed religion had held an honoured place in the curriculum. Indeed, unlike some of the continental universities, most British universities had a Christian and not a rationalist foundation, though that had little influence in the twentieth century.

Grass-roots Christian life

The majority of the population had, by today's standards, a considerable knowledge of the elements of Christian faith and morals. This came from a substantial biblical content in religious education in schools and attendance of very large numbers at Sunday schools. Christian morality was generally accepted as the norm, even when it was not practised, and as a result most people had some sense of being sinners. Evangelism was therefore usually rather blunt. Open-air preaching was common, though not very fruitful. Even the relatively academic Cambridge Inter-Collegiate Christian Union (CICCU) was holding regular open-airs up to 1939.

The 1662 Prayer Book was universally used in Anglican churches,[18] and that brought the gospel in the clearest terms to innumerable parishioners. Its plain acceptance that we are all sinners by nature as well as in deed, that we cannot 'presume to come to this thy Table . . . trusting in our own righteousness, but in thy manifold and great mercies', because Jesus had 'made . . . (by his one oblation of himself once offered) a full, perfect, and sufficient sacrifice, oblation, and satisfaction, for the sins of the whole world' must have had great influence on enormous numbers of people.

The grassroots situation of the CE cause was by no means altogether discouraging. There was an older generation of stalwarts in all the denominations. The scattered evangelical churches, however, had few links between them. The Church Pastoral Aid Society provided finance for curates in evangelical parishes, and the Anglican patronage system gave continuity in churches so that they could build up a strong training programme of young people, though some of the main evangelical trusts, such as the Simeon Trust, were in firmly LE hands. In the other churches it was harder to maintain a continuity of CE ministry as there were not enough theologically astute lay leaders to influence new appointments. The Methodist system did not allow that sort of continuity and Methodist evangelicals suffered accordingly. Evangelical ministers in denominational churches tended to play no part in denominational affairs and to be as independent of the official leadership as possible. They did not want to get involved in disputes, and in any case were usually not well equipped to do so.

The Children's Special Service Mission (CSSM, now Scripture Union) did a very effective work, with its daily Bible-reading schemes, beach missions and camps, staffed largely by lay people. These tended in those years to reach the middle-class and reading public almost exclusively. The same was true of the Crusaders' Unions (also staffed mainly by lay people), which supplied many of the future leaders and a large number of missionaries. In 1938 there was an average attendance of 10,000 in boys' Crusader classes and 6,000 in girls' classes each week, as well as about half that number again attending sometimes.[19] Many of these were not from church-going families. The National Young Life Campaign did a fine work, reaching also the less educated, with city-wide evangelistic rallies in the largest halls available, schools of evangelism and local fellowship groups.[20] The NYLC pioneered 'holiday conventions' at this time, and Frederick P. Wood, one of the founders and the chief evangelist, has been described as the 'Billy Graham' of that generation. The city missions, notably the London City Mission and the Irish Church Missions, along with the Salvation Army, did valiant and fruitful work in depressed areas. Numerous Baptist and independent churches carried on a solid work, with good youth organizations such as the Boys' and Girls' Brigades and, especially in Ireland, Christian Endeavour. People were being converted and made strong in faith. There was much really sacrificial service and funding for Christian mission at home and abroad.

There were, however, far fewer flourishing evangelical churches than today, though some had large congregations gathered from a wide area. In fact many of the best-known churches were distinctively liberal, such as those of Leslie Weatherhead (the City Temple) and Donald Soper (Kingsway Hall) in London; and there were some strong LE churches such as Holy Trinity in Cambridge.

Evangelical ministers were often isolated and easily discouraged when things were tough. The bishops, superintendents and others who were meant to help them were very rarely sympathetic. Even the relatively orthodox Irish church leadership was practically never in the hands of people who wanted to be thought of as evangelicals. Evangelicals felt that they were discriminated against (and often they were), though it was partly their own fault because they played so little part in the life of the denominations. Many Anglicans behaved as if they were in a congregational church, ignoring the authorities as far as possible. Such a course of action was easier to adopt at that time, as there was little episcopal control, and it had considerable theological justification. In the circumstances it seemed a necessary strategy. In the 1990s it is sometimes spoken against as if there was something disreputable about it, though it has of course an honourable history. Some have argued that too much involvement in the denomination in Presbyterian and some Baptist circles, as well as later in Anglican circles, has weakened clear evangelical witness, left individual congregations and their ministers too vulnerable to the eclectic pressures of a mixed denomination, and muted their public voice for evangelical truth.

In *Wales*, apart from the work of the Brethren, a few Pentecostal churches in South Wales and a very few strong individuals, there was very little CE ministry. In view of the 1904 revival this is surprising, but that movement had come to a rather abrupt end. Its lack of much doctrinal substance and its emphasis on experience had left the churches very vulnerable to liberal influence from the colleges, even though there were still many older people who had been converted in the revival. Nantlais Williams, a Presbyterian who had been converted in 1904 (after ordination), and R. B. Jones, a Baptist who owed much to the revival, were among a very few strong CE ministers.[21] (Williams and a colleague were charged with 'Bible worship, shackled minds and tyrannizing' when they successfully prevented a very liberal revision of the Confession of Faith of their church.) The main evangelical conferences and the one or two Bible schools were of a rather subjective Keswick or Adventist tradition which failed to answer the prevailing liberalism. As far back as 1925, some CEs were already despairing of the Welsh denominations and thinking of possible independent churches. Liberals were already seeking some fresh inspiration in exploring the Celtic tradition.[22]

In 1927, Dr Martyn Lloyd-Jones had come to Aberavon as the minister straight from his medical practice in London, and had begun to emerge increasingly as a leader of the evangelical cause in Wales. Even though he moved back to London in 1938, his influence continued to be extensive, especially because he preached as outstandingly in Welsh as in English.[23]

In *Ireland*, many of the Anglicans were helped by the Irish Church Missions, which was led by T. C. Hammond until 1936, and was involved in effective but sometimes dangerous outreach to the Roman Catholic community. Hammond was unique. Starting work at thirteen as a railway clerk in Cork, he was much involved in open-air witness. He managed to get into Trinity College, Dublin, to train for the Church of Ireland ministry, ending with several prizes including the gold medal for philosophy. Many Catholics, including a number of priests, were converted through him. Full of Irish humour and quick in repartee in debate, he became a leading doctrinal teacher and controversialist. Although he was, for a time, on an IRA hit-list, he was spared in recognition of his cross-denominational relief work. Interestingly, in spite of its faults, he normally used the RC-approved Douay version of the Bible in discussion and debate with Catholics, because he could show them the *imprimatur* of the Catholic Primate and so persuade them to read it when Protestant versions were banned.

Ireland was much more religious than the rest of the British Isles. Church attendance was higher and evangelism continuous, much of it in the old revival tradition, with repeated appeals to decision and consecration. Explicit liberalism had bitten into church life later in Ireland than in the rest of the British Isles. It had begun to influence the younger ministers through their theological training, but most remained rather staid and fairly orthodox, though with little evangelical fire.

In *Scotland* too, church attendance was high, and (as in Ireland) there were no defined parties in the main denominations. The Baptist cause in both countries was very small, though in England and Wales the Baptists had some very strong congregations, which, to their credit, reached mainly a less-educated population than did the larger denominations. The latter was true of the Pentecostal churches also.

Much of the best work nationwide was in fact being done by the Brethren.[24] They were proportionately much stronger within evangelicalism then they are today, and frequently had an excellent outreach as well as a very remarkable missionary record, which they still maintain. They did not hit the headlines, partly because they had no ministers; but in numerous evangelistic and missionary organizations the leadership was largely Brethren and evangelical Anglican (and Presbyterian in Scotland and Ireland). Many of the early leaders in Crusaders and the university CUs, for instance, were Brethren. Some of the finest children's evangelists, such as Hudson Pope, and some outstanding Bible teachers at conferences, such as Harold St John, were Brethren, and they provided models for others. They commonly had an exceptional knowledge of the Bible and they read and studied it avidly. They had excellent devotional emphases, but little systematic theology beyond the basics.

Weaknesses

One result of all this was that, feeling marginalized by others, evangelical churches had developed a *defensiveness* and often a traditionalism about them. If they were to keep the faith, it seemed necessary to do it as their forebears had done. The liberals and LEs were more adventurous, but diluted the message in doing so. Many evangelicals, especially in the Anglican churches, still saw their chief opponents as the high-church party. This led them to define their position negatively in terms of ritual rather than doctrine in many contexts. There was much debate about clerical dress, position at the communion table and the finer points of the communion service, all of which carried doctrinal implications but did not seem very important to the unchurched.

There was also a strong tendency to *legalism* about conduct. Drink, tobacco, the cinema and theatre, make-up and dancing were all generally taboo. DJ used to relate how, as a schoolboy with an uncertain conscience, he dared to go to a theatre. When he was met by a notice saying 'To the Pit', he decided that he must make his rapid escape! No responsible evangelical would be seen going into a pub, though pubs were admittedly very different from what they are today. Relationships between the sexes were extremely restrained. In fact it was difficult for young people to get to know one another, as 'going out' was frowned on unless it was already 'serious'. This made people easy prey to less inhibited non-Christians. The trouble was that these things were held to constitute 'worldliness', and became a test of orthodoxy, or at least of what constituted a 'keen Christian'.

Like all legalisms, this outlook made it easy to be complacent about more subtle forms of worldliness. It also tended to isolate evangelicals from much social and cultural life, and pushed many of the more adventurous spirits into non-evangelical circles. Here they were liable to be told that evangelicalism was fine for getting you converted, but if you wanted to live in the real world you had to grow out of it. Many of the more thoughtful young people did just that, and supplied in the next generation some of the ablest and most spiritual leadership in other theological traditions.

There was generally among CEs something of an intellectual inferiority complex and a negative attitude to contemporary 'high' culture. This helped to produce an *anti-intellectualism* that was fed by seeing some promising people turned away from the old paths by wider interests. The older leaders often advised people (including myself) not to read theology because it never seemed to do anyone any good unless they positively needed it for the ministry. When, as a first-year science student, I mentioned my interest in current poetry (T. S. Eliot and W. H. Auden), I was told that it would be best not to broadcast it or I would be thought by some to be 'unsound'. At the same time it has to be remembered that the majority of the population had left school at fourteen and gone straight into a six-days-a-week job. Sundays were busy and there was a rich popular Christian culture revolving round the then numerous mission halls (some of them Anglican) and downtown churches. That culture was nearer to the culture of their neighbours than a smattering of 'high' culture would have been, and it helped them in evangelism.

Evangelicalism did not produce a ghetto mentality, but it did tend to a too-circumscribed outlook that could seem oppressive to those who had access to wider thinking. As very few young people from Baptist and Independent churches went to university or left their home town, those churches were able to continue their work without being aware of the problems. In England, the Anglicans in particular lost many of the children of evangelical families when they went to university or in other ways broadened their intellectual interests. It was observed that a high proportion of those who were being converted came to faith in their teens. It was harder to reach older non-Christians as the gap between them and CEs widened almost into two cultures.

The pacifist issue illustrates the situation. When conscription arrived in 1938 after Munich, it was a hot question. In all the discussion about pacifism in evangelical circles, however, there was very little discussion of a doctrine of the state. Few evangelicals had articulate views in such areas. John Stott, who was a student in Cambridge from 1939 to 1945, says that it was this absence of a real doctrine of the state that seemed to make pacifism necessary at that stage. This was no doubt reinforced by the fact that Dr Basil Atkinson, a strong New Testament Greek scholar who was on the staff of the university library, had great influence in the Cambridge CU. He was a staunch pacifist, though he did not press his view. It was known that he had been in prison in the First World War for his pacifism. As a slightly eccentric bachelor with time to give to numerous college Bible studies, he was much respected, though he was also the healthy butt of numerous jokes. He was the only senior member of the university to support the CU openly, and cultivated the leadership to good effect when they were under various pressures to compromise. He was, however, a linguist rather than a theologian or a doctrinally deep thinker. His sometimes superficial answers to questions were at times counter-productive.[25]

E. J. H. Nash (always known as 'Bash') similarly represented some of the best in the leaders as well as some of the weaknesses.[26] An Anglican clergyman, he concentrated on camps for boys from the top public schools, did a very effective evangelistic work, and gave the 'Bash Campers' a marvellous grounding in basic doctrine and godly discipline. A number of future leaders, such as John Stott, Roland Lamb and Michael Green, were converted through this work and owed much to him. Others were drawn in to be officers at the camps, and John Wenham was one who acknowledged his debt to Bash for the excellent basic training as a camp officer. But Bash was always frightened of the dangers of going 'intellectual'. He stressed the 'simple gospel' and was very wary of the IVF and its interest in apologetics and deeper doctrine. As a result, many of his campers had to break free, and not all of them remained orthodox in doing so. When John Wenham became active in the IVF, Bash felt he had been 'spoiled'. Later in life he began to see the importance of such interests, but at the height of his influence he did not.

One consequence was that very few CEs rose to positions of high responsibility in their professions. If one of them was appointed even as a head teacher in a state school, it was regarded as quite an event. But in fact not many would have been very good at holding high office, because their perspectives were too narrowly focused on evangelism and basic teaching. This, of course, had its positive side. If they saw themselves, with some justification, as the defenders of orthodoxy with their backs to the wall, then they needed to concentrate on essentials. In so doing, they laid strong foundations for future advances, but they bequeathed the real danger of a life in which there was little connection between their church activities and their working life.

CEs of that time had serious weaknesses. Preoccupied with children's work and basic teaching, which they did well, they rarely did enough to develop more work among older Christians or to help them to apply the faith to other than basic personal morality. They also ran the risk of pride, because they felt that they were keeping to Scripture when others were not. Prebendary H. W. Hinde, the Principal of Oak Hill College, wrote in 1935 (in a book published by the IVF!) that, although he greatly valued the help that he had received as a member of the CU in Cambridge, there was a danger in the IVF of 'lacking a becoming humility' and a 'certain intolerance'. This was not confined to students.[27] There must have been some truth in this, though what looked like arrogance to older people like Hinde was partly a new confidence in biblical doctrine that made the rising young leaders willing to call the bluff of the establishment and so to appear cheeky or rude to the authorities. The CEs were far from being paragons of virtue. They had their sins as well as their weaknesses, which makes the fact of God's blessing on their work all the more remarkable. They were often too censorious of others and too quick to dismiss as hopeless any they thought not quite 'sound', seeing no good at all in what they wrote or thought. The battle lines were too tightly drawn.

The intense activism of evangelicals meant that they were suspicious of more meditative forms of worship. This drove some of their members, who felt that evangelicals had lost this aspect of worship, into the high-church tradition. Evangelical churches were also so busy with numerous mid-week activities and missionary causes that there was little time for friendly contact with non-Christians.

It is easy, and rather popular today, to give a very negative picture of the CEs of this period. Randle Manwaring, for instance, writes that 'In their earlier days, members of the IVF had little use for the established church, they eschewed involvement in society, they tended to be life-denying rather than life-affirming, and they had little culture.'[28] (He must mean 'high culture'.) If this may have been partly true of some of the rank and file, because that was their church upbringing, it was not true of most of the leaders, such as Douglas Johnson (DJ), Harold Earnshaw-Smith and Hugh R. Gough (Smith and Gough being the first two travelling secretaries of the IVF, part-time). Though evangelical Anglicans and Presbyterians had no great concern for the structures of the churches or the official leadership, they were usually very loyal to their local congregation and often went on to ordination. Hugh Gough in fact became Archbishop of Sydney, and Harold Earnshaw-Smith was the influential Rector of All Souls, Langham Place, London, before John Stott (who started as his curate). The IVF's first woman staffworker, Jean Strain, married the editor of the IVF magazine – one Donald Coggan. As well as later being the wife of the Archbishop of Canterbury, she has had a wide-ranging ministry in churches and in other circles right up to and beyond his retirement. Many early IVF members were also active in downtown missions in the big cities while they were students. Randle Manwaring's judgment therefore does not seem to be totally accurate.

Evangelism and apologetics

The confidence that evangelicals had in the superiority of God's revelation to all human wisdom is so foundational that it was pure gain to maintain it.

What was a serious weakness was their failure at this stage to grapple with the modern mind in a biblical way. The chief reason was that their theological tools were weak. If you do not have a well-developed framework of biblical theology you are at a loss in apologetics, applied theology and ethics. This also largely explains the legalism and anti-intellectualism of this period. In the absence of a biblical approach to the world of thought and ethics you are forced to run away from debate and to replace New Testament ethics, which is always based on doctrine, by mere rules. Those theological thinkers who professed to be grappling with modern thought had generally been too deeply influenced by what they were facing, and had compromised the faith in order to make it more acceptable. CEs in particular therefore tended to avoid the task.

There was only one substantial evangelical voice heard in Britain calling for what we would now term a Christian mind. The concept was not in wide use, but Daniel Lamont, the Professor of Practical Theology at Edinburgh, published his *Christ and the World of Thought* in 1934.[29] He also spoke under the same title at the big IVF international student conference in Cambridge in the summer of 1939. This gathering (organized by DJ) laid the foundations for the creation of the International Fellowship of Evangelical Students after the war, and attracted 900 students from thirty-three countries. The two main British speakers were Lamont and Lloyd-Jones, who were both to be major factors in the recovery of CE intellectual and theological confidence and vision.[30] Incidentally, that conference provided a remarkable intercommunion service of a kind that the World Council of Churches could not achieve, with Anglican, Lutheran, Reformed and Russian Orthodox ministers all taking part and with the permission of the bishop! The Russian was Dr V. Ph. Martinovski, who had been a leader in the Russian SCM.

Evangelical activism at that time meant almost exclusively evangelistic activity at home and abroad. Evangelism, however, tended to be very direct. Moody and Sankey still provided a model for many. Open-air preaching in Hyde Park or with the city mission halls and the Irish Church Missions often gave people their first experience of evangelism. Even the children's work could be too forceful in asking for decisions. Bash and a few others were more cautious from long experience, and encouraged what we might now call friendship evangelism. CEs were often bold but tactless. According to his biographer, A. M. Ramsey, the future Archbishop, never quite forgave the students in the CU who had brought in Willy Nicholson as their missioner in a combined university mission in Cambridge in 1926 when he was a student.[31] Ramsey always thought of CEs as unintellectual and emotional, and that was a not uncommon picture of them in the minds of others. It was also not totally undeserved, though it was a caricature. Nicholson was, of course, an extreme. He had a very rough and blunt style in the old revivalist tradition. He had a remarkable ministry, especially among working-class people in Ireland, and many of his converts went on to the ministry or the mission field. In Cambridge he certainly saw some conversions; but introducing him into a university mission alienated some of the more thoughtful, while it strengthened the conviction of the CEs that straightforward evangelism was far more effective than the learned apologetics of the other speakers. The leading IVF evangelist in the 1930s was Howard Guinness (a doctor). He was reputed to have driven his motorbike into Bart's Hospital grounds, when he was a student, with the words 'Prepare to meet thy God' in large letters on the front. If the story is not certainly true, it is not impossible.

Apologetics was usually handled badly by evangelicals. Some of it was so simplistic as to be counter-productive. DJ brought into the IVF some good people from the world of medicine. Professor Rendle Short had a wide ministry, as did Professor Duncan Blair and others to a lesser extent. Blair liked to relate how, when he was Professor of Anatomy at Kings College, London, he was approached by a chubby medical student (DJ) who asked if it was true that he was an elder in the Free Church of Scotland. If so, did he believe in the Westminster Confession – all of it? If so, would he take the chair at the next CU meeting? Blair acknowledged that this was a major step forward in his Christian life, as he had never before taken a stand as a Christian in front of his students. He became a frequent speaker at conferences.

The Victoria Institute tried to tackle some of the issues in apologetics, but had only a small circle of readers. Most of the literature in this area was out of date. T. C. Hammond, with his books and his training programmes in Ireland, Rendle Short, who wrote on science and the Bible, and Daniel Lamont, were making a more effective contribution.

IVF books by these and other authors were beginning to have some real influence. H. E. Guillebaud's *Why the Cross?* (1937) clarified this key doctrine for many readers. The most influential book was T. C. Hammond's *In Understanding be Men* (1936, and still in print in revised form in the late 1990s).[32] It described itself as 'A handbook of Christian doctrine for non-theological students', but it influenced many future leaders and ministers. It also gave many their first systematic view of biblical doctrine as a whole – what has been described recently as 'the Bible's plot line'. The particular parts make far greater sense when seen in the context of 'a comprehensive story that provides the framework for a comprehensive explanation'. Hammond helped evangelicals to recover that sense of the unity of revealed truth and so to be gripped by doctrine. It opened a new world of biblical doctrine to many readers. The idea for the book seems to have been DJ's, and he spent days going over to Dublin working with Hammond to complete the main draft before Hammond left for Australia, DJ polishing it largely himself. I myself and Dr Robin Wells, my successor as General Secretary of the UCCF, both acknowledge a substantial debt to the book read while we were students, as do a remarkable number of others.

John Wenham had a genius for placing books with key people, including the best of B. B. Warfield and Gresham Machen, the older American theological giants (though to me as a scientist he gave Lamont's *Christ and the World of Thought*). These and other USA Reformed writers had considerable circulation in Ulster through the Evangelical Bookshop, which gave them a prominent place.

Generally, evangelicals were rather frightened of the intellectual climate. A not untypical medical student, starting in London in 1934, was told by her headmistress that her faith could not stand up at university. She arrived, she says, 'frightened . . . but delighted to find a small but convinced group of believers. The CU members certainly had their backs to the wall, adopted a largely defensive position and ganged together with few cross-cultural friendships.'[33] She and they, however, survived, had their faith strengthened and went on to have a considerable evangelistic influence after the war, providing some fine writers and speakers.

Spiritual life

At a personal level the discipline of a daily 'quiet time' of Bible reading and prayer was universally pressed upon young and old alike in evangelical circles. It too could become a little legalistic, but it was widely practised and was in fact the main spiritual diet for many who did not have access to a good church. Scripture Union notes were widely used in CE circles, and the Bible Reading Fellowship notes in LE and some other groups. CEs regarded the latter as too 'critical'. Both were fairly superficial, and in 1934 the IVF introduced a much more demanding series, taking the reader through the whole Bible in three years, with questions rather than short devotional commentaries. *Search the Scriptures*, by G. T. Manley, H. E. Guillebaud and others, was widely used by students and others. It is still in print in revised form in 1997. Those who worked through the Bible in this way certainly gained greatly from it. It was especially a gain for those whose quiet time had, as one student expressed it, been judged by 'the gooey feeling that you got inside'.

As the King James (Authorized) Version of the Bible was used in almost all churches, its phrases were generally known, and learning verses by heart was a common practice with young and old alike. Preachers and teachers could refer to a verse confident that it could be hammered home in memorable terms. What it said carried authority, and many non-Christians knew a good many Bible phrases and verses. As the *Book of Common Prayer* was used rigidly in all Anglican churches, except the most extreme Anglo-Catholic parishes, the Creed was recited and the Psalms were sung each Sunday by thousands of nominal Christians.

Keswick had great influence on the devotional life of CEs. It provided a focus for evangelical forces (more than the Evangelical Alliance). It went across denominational boundaries, meeting under the banner 'All One in Christ Jesus', and local 'Keswicks' or similar 'conventions' were held in several regions. It was a standard-bearer of devotional Bible ministry and missionary commitment, but at that time it had a strong, though not exclusive, emphasis on a second stage of sanctification after a first stage of salvation. Its emphasis could be summed up in the exhortation, 'You have accepted Christ as your Saviour; now make him also your Lord.' There was a good deal of stress on 'full surrender' before a Christian could make any progress in holiness. Keswick had shed its extremes of the past, and its voice in the weekly magazine *The Life of Faith* and the published Keswick Bible readings were widely appreciated as giving better ministry than was available in many churches. It was solidly biblical, though rather narrow in its doctrinal range, and at that stage inclined to be too introspective. It did not help people to think doctrinally, but concentrated on devotional life and missionary stimulus. Although it helped to unite and steady the CEs, it was too preoccupied with what *we* can *receive* in the way of inner 'blessings' to give a lead in the coming evangelical recovery.

The China Inland Mission (now OMF International), which had strong links with Keswick, together with other 'faith' missions (including the home missions of the Faith Mission, especially in Scotland and Ireland), provided a model of spirituality. A great deal of energy was spent in discussions of various theories of the second coming of Christ, and, though the disputes were not very profitable, they did keep this New Testament emphasis in the forefront of evangelical thinking.

There was a deep current of warm spiritual life fed by the constant input of the Bible in many different church traditions. It expressed itself in sacrificial service and, in evangelical circles, especially in evangelistic activity and generous giving.

Social action

Evangelicals, especially CEs, usually held a negative view of social action in the name of Christianity – that is to say, social action within Britain other than philanthropy. There is an unclear line between philanthropy and attempts to alter the structures of society for the better. On the mission field they could not easily avoid going beyond philanthropy, and they were deeply involved in medical and educational work and in other programmes with a social dimension. With few exceptions, however, social action at home was regarded as a dangerous distraction from 'gospel work'. George Müller's orphanages and the political campaigns of Wilberforce and Shaftesbury were admired, but their example was rarely followed. This was partly a reaction against the 'social-gospel' tradition of the liberals and the perception that social action replaced evangelism in many churches because they had lost their priorities. It was sometimes said by CEs that while the liberals talked about the social applications of Christianity, they themselves were concerned with its personal applications. With some chagrin I remember describing the difference between the CU and the SCM in those terms when I was a student. It was an over-reaction, but when the biblical gospel seemed to be in danger of being eclipsed by liberal and high-church theology, social action seemed to be a diversion, especially when it was largely theoretical and had little practical outlet. Basic local philanthropy was at least providing help to many, and much of that went on unnoticed.

Some of the downtown medical missions, such as the Lansdown Place Medical Mission in London's East End (in which the indefatigable DJ was medical officer for a time), the Salvation Army, the city missions and some of the congregations in depressed areas were faced with the duty of meeting acute needs, and did so generously. The idea that evangelicals should work to alter the structures of society and make them more just was, however, held by many CEs to be inappropriate. Certainly it was held to be inappropriate for the churches to act politically as churches, and there was doubt about whether individuals should be deeply involved. In some Brethren circles, particularly in Ireland, there was even doubt as to whether a Christian should vote. The Scofield Bible and a premillennial view of the second coming of Christ, which were specially influential in Brethren circles, gave reasons for thinking that society would inevitably get worse and that it was futile to try to improve it.

There were CEs involved in politics (as the 1920s Prayer Book debates had shown), but their numbers were very small, and they rarely (if ever) spoke or wrote about a Christian approach to political action.

Missionary concerns

There was no hesitation, however, about missionary work and action. Great sacrifices were made in this area. Not only was missionary service still quite costly in terms of life expectancy and certainly in terms of career, but great efforts were made to raise money and recruits for it. The largest societies held annual meetings in London attended by enthusiastic audiences of over a thousand. Middle-class people curtailed luxuries, had economical holidays and held working parties to raise money for missions. Really poor people put a missionary box on the mantelpiece for any spare pennies, and many well-off people, some from aristocratic families, went as missionaries in an honorary capacity. To be a missionary was regarded as the highest spiritual achievement. In fact, the missionary and the minister at home were exalted to such a position that no other occupation was thought comparable. There was hardly any positive vision for other tasks as a vocation, except perhaps medicine. To go by choice into business or industry or law could be regarded as suspect. At least it was regarded as second best, except in Brethren circles where there were few openings for what was often called 'full-time Christian work' in the UK.

The IVF and the Crusaders' Unions had a remarkable missionary record. By 1934 the small IVF already knew of 295 former members of CUs abroad[34] as missionaries; the Girl Crusaders' Union knew of 563 by 1958. Several of the senior leaders of CE theological thinking were returned missionaries. G. T. Manley, H. E. Guillebaud and Alan Stibbs were all missionaries home for various reasons. They had learned in pioneer situations that it was essential to work from the Bible, and that what 'seemed reasonable' or what 'I believe' was of no importance. Some of the LE leaders were forced to adopt the same position abroad, and modified their ministry when they came home. This shift of perspective was also beginning to apply more at home as the background consensus of Christian ideas began to crumble.

Renewal movements

The interwar years had been years of great heart-searching in the churches. They had lost much of their popular support. Committed membership and church attendance were declining, and their influence in the nation was clearly much less than before 1914. There had therefore been a serious search for new initiatives that might rekindle the flame of faith in the churches and in the country as a whole.[35]

These movements did not think that the churches could be revived by a return to the 'old-fashioned' traditions or stress on doctrine. They looked for something distinctively new. There was a widespread belief that in order to progress, one must abandon some old certainties, break free from denominational ties and find a new spirituality. The Bible and the cross were prominent at first in these movements, but in a much less clear sense than before. Fresh experience of Christ and a fresh spirituality were sought in listening to God in silence, helped by conferences, retreats and conventions that were not dominated by the Bible.

The *Keswick* movement was different from the developments I shall mention below because it tried at all costs to keep to the Bible. It also was looking for renewal but in an experience of fresh inner sanctification and consecration. The three other main movements, however, were all to cut free from an exclusive stress on the Bible as the source of doctrine and the measure of new experiences. In so doing they moved progressively away from biblical orthodoxy and a strong biblical diet. These movements were in part a reaction to what was perceived as the aridity and defensiveness of the orthodox churches, including many CEs.

The *Oxford Group*, which was usually known as Moral Rearmament (MRA) after 1938, had been started in the early 1920s by an American Lutheran minister, Frank Buchman, under the title 'First Century Christian Fellowship'.[36] He had a revolutionary experience at the 1908 Keswick Convention and concentrated at first on working with students. By the 1930s he led an influential body, convening conferences of 5,000 in 1933 and 1934, and a two-day event of 25,000 in 1936. It has been described by a historian of the period as 'an expression of proto-charismatic spirituality'.[37] It had, in common with early Quakerism and later charismatic movements, a stress on direct and authoritative words from God to the individual, and an experience of Christ without the 'interference' of reason, church or Bible. It did not stress 'charismatic gifts', visions or dreams, but it had a stress on what would now be called prophecy and on the thoughts revealed to the individual in quiet contemplation and openness to God. These were 'guidance', and were to be written down and shared with others. Group quiet times could lead to a consensus that someone's guidance was God's word for the whole group. Sometimes it was guidance for others to do this or that, and such guidances could be contradictory. Its greatest success was in Oxford. Teams of students went out on evangelistic missions in towns and villages. 'The Groups' were welcomed across a wide theological spectrum as a movement of spiritual revival, and many LEs were involved. It was a breath of fresh air and undoubtedly challenged sleepy or lazy Christians to fresh 'surrender'. Early on, it had the virtue of emphasizing a supernatural Christianity, and talked of 'the age of miracles' having returned. It stressed the need to bring others to surrender their lives to Christ and to follow four absolutes: absolute honesty, purity, unselfishness and love, which easily lapsed into a doctrinally empty moralism. In fact, the change of name to Moral Rearmament represented a big shift in emphasis.

At first it was clearly a CE movement and stressed the work of the Holy Spirit and the creation of a vibrant Christian fellowship with evangelistic drive. Initially it had links with Keswick, and its emphasis on 'surrender' was not totally dissimilar. It soon moved away from Keswick, however, and revolved round a small group of leaders, especially Buchman. Those who disagreed with him left. It became decreasingly Bible-based, and in the late 1930s was a good deal concerned with combating communism. David Bebbington emphasizes that 'the Groups' wanted to bypass reason in receiving messages from God in the quiet time. He correctly points out that this was to be a feature of other streams of evangelicalism, especially some charismatic elements, later on. It was, however, the bypassing of the Bible that was to do most damage and that warned CEs not to get involved. One of the members of the CICCU committee described how, after long discussion, they decided that 'if we aligned ourselves with the Oxford Groups we would in the end undermine the strong CICCU stand on biblical doctrine'.[38] Buchman had preached for them and given a Bible study over a weekend.

The introduction of authoritative guidance from God direct to leaders and apart from the Bible has of course been the foundation of almost all cults. Although the young CICCU leaders were probably not thinking of that, they were given a remarkable discernment that something was not right about the movement – which is why Buchman moved to Oxford, where he had more success. It was, however, hailed by less discerning people as the beginning of revival.

Undoubtedly 'the groups' helped some people to a more wholehearted and disciplined faith. As long as people's thoughts were soaked in biblical truth, the style of quiet time did not seem to be too dangerous, but as time went on the difficulties multiplied. 'Guidance' gradually replaced personal Bible study and had to be checked with others. People with very little biblical background could come up with strange ideas. Strong leadership controls had to be introduced. As often happens, a boasted freedom needs some kind of authority to prevent it drifting into chaos.

There are interesting comparisons with Quakerism. When the Quakers were soaked in the Bible and read it avidly, they were an evangelical movement in most respects (and there are still evangelical Quakers in some parts, especially in the USA and Northern Ireland). Their doctrine of the 'inner light' was not the same as the Oxford Group/MRA's 'guidance', but it had many of the same virtues and dangers. When they have been relying on the Bible they have compared favourably with much dry and formal religion. Their principle has, however, allowed them easily to drift away from the Bible and rely on 'prophets' and those who have an inner conviction or concern. Then they have quickly ceased to be evangelical and, like the Oxford Group, give an almost exclusive priority to ethical responsibilities. That is very worthy, but does not make them evangelical. It is another case of a loss of biblical input leading to a drift away from biblical priorities. When, in the later nineteenth century,[39] the drift away from a conservative position gathered strength, many of the more strongly biblical Quakers left and joined the Brethren, where they formed a not inconsiderable group of Brethren stalwarts. It is told of one of the Quaker leaders that, carrying a Bible under his arm to meeting, he was reproved for not relying more on the immediate inspiration of the Holy Spirit. This led him to join the Brethren. In the same way, a good many who had at first been helped by the Oxford Group pulled out when it became less biblical, looking for a better diet.

Buchman rarely spoke directly from a Bible passage because, he said, he feared that that would put people off. The lack of much real biblical input began to tell, and the movement became more strongly political. At first, a number of IVF supporters were drawn in and there were attempts to get the IVF to become part of it. Efforts to capture particular student CUs also failed, after drawing away a few leaders. Julian Thornton-Duesberry, who had been the first Secretary of the IVF conference for one year (1923–24) before handing it over to DJ, became a life-long Group/MRA supporter. As he was to become Master of St Peter's Hall, Oxford, and then Principal of Wycliffe Hall, Oxford, he became an important influence. The movement's adherents included the Professor of the Philosophy of Religion at Oxford (L. E. Grensted), and a number of people who were later to be influential as somewhat liberal evangelical leaders in the Church of England and outside it. These included Cuthbert Bardsley, who was later to be the Bishop of Coventry, and the future Church of Scotland Evangelist, D. P. Thomson.[40]

The emphasis on 'life-changing', however, became more and more vague. By 1939 'the Groups' were losing ground and attracting evangelicals of all kinds less and less. They had failed to accomplish what had been hoped. Their almost anti-doctrinal stance, in favour of the experience of 'life-changing' and 'surrender', undermined their original evangelical emphases and left them with too little substance.

Two other movements, surveyed below, were also seeking renewal in direct and uncluttered access to God, but were both dominated by the conviction that to make Christianity plausible to the new generation it was necessary to make concessions to liberal biblical criticism and modern thought.

The *Fellowship of the Kingdom* was a movement within Methodism.[41] Started in 1919, it was always overwhelmingly a ministerial group. In the 1930s it was still strong. It had been a force for evangelistic campaigns ('crusades') supported by retreats, where 'waiting upon God' was prominent. Theological clarity was blurred in 'the Quest', which was a major element. It was a quest for spiritual experience and renewed evangelistic zeal through introspective experience helped by conferences and fellowship. It distanced itself from traditional Methodism, often stating that there could be no progress by going back to biblical doctrines that were not acceptable to the modern mind. Ian Randall describes one of its aims: 'Methodism had to be remoulded along what was being termed "liberal evangelical" lines.' Conversion was not seen so much in terms of being saved; 'the Quest' was for an as yet undefined 'experience of Christ'. Speakers from other traditions, including the Oxford Group and very high-church circles, were on the platform at conferences. It had at its peak included about one fifth of all Methodist ministers. By the late 1930s it was weakening in influence, though still strong in numbers. It did not produce the revival of the church that had been hoped, and in some ways encouraged the doctrinal looseness that became a mark of much Methodism after the war. By 1955 its *Bulletin* sharply criticized Billy Graham's theology. There was in fact something of a polarization within Methodism. At the CE end were the Southport Convention and Cliff College, in the 'holiness' tradition; and at the other was the Fellowship of the Kingdom, which looked back neither to Wesley nor primarily to the Bible.[42]

In Anglican circles the corresponding movement was the *Anglican Evangelical Group Movement* (AEGM), formed in 1923. This was glad of the description 'liberal evangelical'.[43] It stressed comprehensiveness. Unlike the more radical Modern Churchmen's Union, with which it had some loose link, it was not primarily a theological movement. Its motto was 'The truth will set you free'. Its emphasis was on an ill-defined experience of Christ. It was said that the new wine of the Spirit will always burst the old wineskins. Oliver Tomkins described it as 'a group of evangelicals who were seeking to revivify evangelicalism with "liberalism" '.[44] Its Cromer Convention was a self-conscious alternative to Keswick. By 1935 it had 1,454 clerical and 187 lay members; that is to say, like the Fellowship of the Kingdom it comprised mostly those who had suffered a liberal theological education. It was led by Canon V. F. Storr, and when he died in 1940 it faded rapidly. The aim was to make the gospel more accessible to the wider world. That involved a departure from the traditional evangelical positions. Although its leaders were constantly reading the Bible and usually had a CE background, the Bible was gradually being replaced by a rather vague and faintly romantic tradition. There was warm fellowship and mutual encouragement. Bible readings at conferences were important. It is not totally unfair, however, to record that whereas Keswick people would go out to the lakeside to pray with their Bibles open, at Cromer the leader of the first convention said that he went up on the cliffs with his 'beloved Wordsworth' in his pocket.[45]

Professor C. E. Raven was a leading speaker. He was Regius Professor of Divinity at Cambridge and a warm and lovable person, who wrote much more effectively on the history of science and faith than on theology.[46] He represents the reasons for AEGM's strengths and weaknesses; when he had spoken, people were moved but not at all clear about what he had said! Having been scornful of CEs, he became more friendly during and after the war, when he recognized the quality of some of his CE theological students.

Having moved away from a frank biblical witness, the AEGM could never quite decide what they did want. When their goal was called 'spirituality', it could not be defined. Although the movement included many extremely warm-hearted and devoted pastors, and provided a helpful fellowship, it was not going anywhere. Like most LEs, they had cut off the branch they were sitting on and had no clear authority for their messages, or great clarity as to what it was.

Many AEGM members became bishops, but mostly soon ceased to be very clearly evangelical. This made William Temple comment, at the consecration of Christopher Chavasse as Bishop of Rochester, that he hoped he would remain an evangelical as 'so many did not'.[47] Chavasse took the advice in his own less than clearly CE way, but whereas most Anglo-Catholics and liberals unashamedly retained their theology when they became bishops, the LEs rarely did. CEs were not being appointed, and few would have been good at the task.

The one exception was the gentle and godly J. R. S. Taylor, the Bishop of Sodor and Man (*i.e.* the Isle of Man).[48]

Liberal disintegration

These three bodies and the decline of the SCM (which I shall mention below) illustrate the fact that evangelical bodies that ceased to maintain a good biblical input soon ceased to be evangelical, whatever else they might become, even if they remained strong for a time in numbers. Liberalism is inevitably an unstable position. If it is to relate to the culture by adaptation of its message, then its message will have to change as the culture changes. Once the principle of adaptation is accepted, it is difficult to know where to stop; many who start on this road become increasingly liberal as time goes on. The LEs on the whole could not prevent an increasing drift away from orthodoxy, even when their evangelical instincts kept them from moving greatly at first.

By 1939 these three movements were showing signs of weakness as they increasingly departed from their biblical roots. In fact, the whole great liberal experiment was beginning to disintegrate, though it took a long time for that to become clear. They were suffering from a growing biblical anaemia. It must be remembered that the leaders of the churches are usually those who went through their theological training twenty or thirty years before. If it is true that many older CEs had not moved from their early positions because they had read little in the meantime, the same was true of many liberals, who continued to rely on the books that had been recommended to them in college.[49] A strong liberal leadership remained prominent in the older generation for a long time, even when at the grass roots it was failing to attract younger people.

This was nowhere more evident than in the *Student Christian Movement* (SCM),[50] which had originally been a clearly CE body. Having moved gradually to a broadly liberal position, it was losing its hold on students, even though it had massive support from university staff and theological faculties. It was no longer certain what it wanted to do or what its message was. It could still put on big events, but their long-term effect on the lives of students was usually small. Archbishop William Temple, who died in 1944, had great influence in the SCM. He tended, however, to recommend programmes more suitable for a ministers' fraternal, and did not push them back to their evangelical roots. One of the SCM's several mistakes (which were easy to make and would be easy to repeat today) had been to concentrate on numbers, even numbers going abroad as missionaries, at the expense of quality. Patronage by church leaders had also been sought, irrespective of what theological baggage they brought with them on to the platform.

At the grass-roots level, liberalism was beginning to fade. The high-church tradition seemed to be as strong as ever in the Anglican churches, though even there the influence of biblical criticism, the results of which were usually taken for granted, were blurring the doctrinal limits.

Meanwhile, the rising young CEs were beginning to be seen as a threat. On the whole they were dismissed as irrational, but in the universities the SCM was increasingly asking the CUs to provide the evangelistic element that they admitted they rather lacked. There was constant pressure for evangelicals to join more in the general theological mish-mash and play their part in the wider life of Christian organizations and churches. These invitations were nearly always firmly rejected, because CEs were unwilling to be just part of an amorphous Christianity, where what they held dear might be repudiated by others and where there was still strong hostility to some of their distinctives. They were aware of the need to build up the faith of young Christians in a consistent manner if they were to stand firm. The experiences of wartime were fully to justify that belief.

At the outbreak of war

At the outbreak of the Second World War, then, evangelicals were divided more sharply than formerly between LEs (who, while often strong numerically, were moving steadily away from evangelical positions) and CEs (who were still generally regarded by others as obsolete). In Anglican churches, the almost dominant high-church party was a strong opponent. In the Free Churches, which had for the most part once been evangelical, liberalism was dominant in stronger or milder forms, though there was a small Baptist Revival Fellowship and a good many individual CE congregations. In the large Presbyterian churches in Scotland and Ireland, there were no clear conservative groupings but a good deal of lively LE ministry, though the term was not much used as a selfconscious label within Presbyterianism. There were, however, vigorous individual CE congregations dotted around, especially in Ireland. The Presbyterian CEs, however, mostly worked closely within the presbyteries, and as a result were not as distinct a body as the Anglican CEs. Whether this increased or weakened their influence can still be debated.

The prospects for evangelicalism did not seem very promising. CEs were numerically weak and often discouraged. LEs were demonstrating the fact that any evangelical body that ceases to maintain a good biblical input will soon cease to be distinctive. It may be strong in numbers and prestige, but it will have too few antibodies to resist error or prevent a drift into vagueness.

Evangelicals in this period could be described as 'pietistic'. The pietist tradition has a great history and has frequently revived dead churches. Often it has kept the gospel alive when official church leadership had largely lost sight of it, and pietists reached the poor better than anyone else. John Wesley owed much to the Moravian pietists with whom he shared a transatlantic voyage. The term has, however, now become a term of abuse in many circles because the pietists did not concern themselves with politics or with improving the structures of society, had little vision for a national official church, and were often rather anti-intellectual. Evangelicals at this time had most of the strengths and weaknesses of an unnecessarily negative pietist tradition.

It is possible, and in many circumstances necessary, to build on a pietistic foundation and add other biblical emphases in an entirely healthy way. It is doubtful, however, if anyone can 'grow out of it' without very serious loss. To do so seems almost inevitably to lead to the preaching of a weakened gospel, and those who attempt this are often unable to reach and to teach young people, even their own children, effectively. We despise a 'simple gospel' at our peril, but there is much more to find in the Bible than that, and we need to discover more than the very basics if we are to know how to live and to witness faithfully to the world around us.

Reasons for weakness

If one could with any confidence discover some of the reasons for the weakness of evangelicalism in the interwar period, it could be a help to us today. CEs were apparently 'stuck' and had been declining in numbers. Any such analysis is provisional, because God, who is the real head of his church, can strengthen it without our help. Nevertheless, in retrospect it is possible to pick out four factors among those mentioned above which seem to have been of greatest importance.

First, CEs neglected theological education and so were dependent on others for it. As a result, many promising ministers and RE teachers ended up as less than clearly evangelical.

Secondly, and consequently, the task of evangelical leadership was taken up largely by people with little depth in biblical doctrine. Good biblical exposition was often replaced by rather superficial devotional material and fanciful interpretations of the Bible.

Thirdly, older leaders were distrustful of theology and inclined to be anti-intellectual. They loved God ardently with heart and strength, but failed to love him with their minds. The most lively, thinking young people in their circle, therefore, often felt restricted or somewhat resentful at the rigidity of the CE traditions, and either moved out, or remained in for a while with a critical spirit. Only a few spoke out in criticism while remaining loyal to the CE community. (I myself well remember an address by one of these, Harold Earnshaw-Smith. Speaking to student leaders in the IVF in 1939 or 1940, he spent most of his time criticizing the backward-looking tendencies of so many evangelicals. No doubt it did us good.) Young people who were exposed to other church traditions or to secular thinking were too vulnerable. As higher education became more widely available, this had increasingly serious implications. The rising new leadership, however, was neither anti-intellectual nor anti-theological. There is often a close link between the two, for a strong biblical theology makes it impossible to believe that error is stronger than God's truth. Lloyd-Jones, G. T. Manley, DJ and others were confident, not because of their intellectual prowess, but because of their theology. The prewar generation (especially the old) were often, in reality, frightened people.

Fourthly, evangelicals in this period too often defined their position negatively and merely defensively, spending too much time attacking others. Not knowing how to tackle issues doctrinally, they tended also to offer simplistic or legalistic solutions. They were against 'worldliness', but did not put a strong, positive view of the good things of God's creation in its place. They were frequently negative about 'high culture', so they did not encourage their young people to a positive view of art and literature. They were often frightened of what science might bring up, and did not urge a positive attitude to scientific knowledge. They tended to be negative about theology, but had hardly any good theological training to offer above an elementary level. They were against high-church practices; in the Church of England they had their own rules of anti-ritual, and in the other churches they tended towards a rather dull worship for fear of compromise. CEs were against social action at home (apart from philanthropy), regarding it as a diversion from evangelism and a dangerous move towards a liberal 'social gospel'. Such negativism led to the alienation of some who would otherwise have been party to a CE position.

Evangelical strengths

The CEs did, however, have great strengths at the grass-roots level. They were keeping alive the gospel when it was frequently being replaced or eclipsed by ritualism, formal religion and liberal semi-humanism. In contrast to many other traditions, there was hardly any dead orthodoxy among them because they were active in evangelism at home and abroad. If they appear in retrospect to have been too tied to their traditional ways, and too negative, they should be respected as the somewhat battle-scarred warriors who had borne the heat of the conflicts and had won enough ground to provide a good base for further advance. They had kept the faith when so many others had not. Evangelical congregations, if not as numerous or as large as today, were often doing a fine work that would be the envy of many in the 1990s. It is always tempting to look back and be too dismissive of that generation – partly in order to boost our own sense of having made progress. This is exemplified, for instance, in some of the books written by evangelicals in 1995,[51] which talk about evangelical ghettoes and narrowness before the war. Honest comparison between the 1930s and today is not altogether in our favour in some very important respects. It is easy to fall into the adolescent habit of dismissing our parents whose basic training we take for granted.

The ordinary members of the CE churches had a knowledge of the Bible that far surpasses ours in the 1990s. They also had a willingness to apply what they found, if need be with a level of self-sacrifice that puts us to shame in our much more comfortable generation that will not risk careers, financial security or comfort. Their vision may have been narrower than ours, but it went deeper in important ways. They would have thought of much modern evangelicalism as dangerously complacent and superficial. They knew that they were in a battle for the gospel nationwide.

Their level of evangelistic and missionary work was admirable. They continued to pour great resources of labour, personnel, money and prayer into the development of the younger churches and the evangelization of virgin territory where the name of Christ was hardly known. This was to bear great fruit worldwide in the second half of the century. There was no lack of vision and confidence in the power of the gospel overseas. At home, however, the older leaders, at least, were forced into a distinctly defensive outlook because they were so small a minority and often under fire. Randle Manwaring described these years as 'The Defensive Years'.[52] Some of that defensiveness was inevitable, but it did not create confidence. A number of the younger evangelical leaders in all denominations did not share that pessimism, and hoped to be able to restore evangelical doctrine and practice to its proper place as at least the main representative of Christianity.

A significant feature of the developments in the next few decades is that they very rarely depended on one or two individuals. Frequently the same concerns were brought into the minds of different people independently. This encouraged those involved to believe that what they were anxious to emphasize was a matter of God's leading them to rediscover things that were clearly biblical but had been lost sight of for a time.

As the subsequent history shows, it was neither those who accommodated the message to the current culture (as in LE circles), nor those who emphasized fresh revelation in direct words from God apart from the Bible (as in the Oxford Group/MRA) who revived the evangelical cause. Those who did so were people who held to its classic core of beliefs with tenacity, but who had shed the remaining anti-intellectualism and suspicion of theology through a recovery of love for biblical doctrine, particularly a renewed doctrine of the Godhead. They were then able to build on the often simple and somewhat pietistic faith in which they had mostly been brought up.

3. THE CRUCIBLE OF WAR 1939–45

All the activities of the churches and societies were of course increasingly curtailed as the war developed. Male leadership in particular was in short supply, and women began to take a more prominent part in Christian work. Life became more serious, and any optimism about the virtues of human nature faded. C. E. M. Joad, a professor of philosophy at London University, who had a high profile on radio and was clearly an unbeliever, announced that he had become a Christian because, he said, he had realized that there was evil deep in the human heart, including his own, and that a drastic remedy was needed. Radio became very important (there was virtually no television). It was extremely rare for CEs to get any opportunities to speak on that medium, though some LEs were popular contributors.

Evangelicals were still treated on the whole with disparagement or scorn. When Lord Rochester was elected Vice-President of the Methodist Conference in 1941, a letter in the religious press complained that 'someone from the backwoods of Methodism' should not have been elected to such high status in the church.[1] He had a great and practical concern for the poor, and was clearly and outspokenly CE, though that title was hardly used in Methodism.

Some excellent work was done among service personnel by churches and missions to the troops. A significant number of future ministers and lay leaders were converted while in uniform, or brought to a more confident faith when all else seemed to be crumbling. Evangelical witness to fellow servicemen and women was tough and often blunt, but faithful, and the lives of Christians and hospitality in Christian homes counted for much.

Missionary work continued under difficulties, but often with official encouragement, since the need for spiritual and moral influences was evident. The Foreign Secretary, Lord Halifax, wrote to the missionary societies encouraging them to keep up their work. Some CE emphases began to seem rather more plausible, though the theological establishment was as strongly opposed as before. People had seen terrible human suffering, and superficial answers were not impressive. The China Inland Mission especially, with its literature and magazine, was a continuing source of spiritual challenge and encouragement to a wide CE public.

A new emphasis on doctrine

The most important development was the convergence of several different influences that emphasized how essential it was for evangelicals, especially CEs, to have a much more doctrinal approach. With this also came a greater confidence that biblical truth could be made influential again, and the determination, by God's grace, to make it so. Douglas Johnson (DJ) was someone of far-sighted vision and extraordinarily hard work. He taught many to love doctrine, and proved the major force in bringing together some of the key people. He and his wife gave generous and costly hospitality to many overseas graduates who were in Britain in the Armed Forces. Thus he laid some of the foundations of what became the International Fellowship of Evangelical Students (IFES), and of other theological developments, after the war. He developed a partnership with A. J. Vereker, the Secretary of the Crusaders' Union,[2] and drew into their plans a number of other formative people including Alan Stibbs, an influential teacher and conference speaker.[3] It was DJ who had persuaded Martyn Lloyd-Jones to speak at the 1935 IVF conference, of which more in a moment.

DJ and Vereker met to fire-watch together during air raids, and planned a number of initiatives. A joint committee of the four related CE youth movements was created, with Vereker as Chairman.[4] DJ never took the chair at anything if he could help it, or appeared on public platforms, but beavered away in the background as Secretary. DJ and Vereker discussed the plan to create a London Bible College, which had been mooted in 1938. The first committee meeting was held in DJ's office at the IVF in 1941, and evening lectures began in London in 1943.[5]

In 1938 and 1939, DJ had convened under G. T. Manley's chairmanship discussions which led, in 1940, to the formal constitution of an IVF Biblical Research Committee. H. E. Guillebaud was the BRC's first Secretary, and members included John Wenham and Alan Stibbs. In 1941, DJ, through the

BRC, drew together a group of like-minded people to plan for serious theological advance at an academic level.[6] They included two theology research students (an Australian and a New Zealander), several working ministers, and Alan Stibbs, with G. T. Manley in the chair. Two theological college principals (Free Church of Scotland and BCMS) were present, but apart from a university lecturer in classics and one in Semitic languages (W. J. Martin), both of them in universities without a theology faculty, there was no-one teaching in a university. Martyn Lloyd-Jones was a major contributor. John Wenham, then a lecturer at the London College of Divinity, was involved, and the classics lecturer was F. F. Bruce, who changed to biblical studies later. No-one had any substantial theological book or even article to his name, but they all were able people determined to change the sad state of conservative theological scholarship. Manley had been top of his year in maths in Cambridge (Senior Wrangler) in the year in which Bertrand Russell had come sixth! He had been a teaching Fellow of Christ's College before going abroad as a missionary with the CMS. While he was now a parish minister, he retained his sharpness of mind and, as chairman of the IVF's Literature Committee, guided its publishing policy. The theological establishment would have dismissed these men as obscurantist. DJ (with a chuckle) often compared the IVF to a group of Boy Scouts with bows and arrows confronting an army of professional soldiers – and scoring some good hits! To all appearances it was an amateurish effort with no resources.

It was clear that, in the face of considerable prejudice, CEs had little chance of gaining ground unless some of them could be helped to do postgraduate work. The universities were not going to support such candidates. They also needed personal help and fellowship if they were to battle through unscathed. The consultation agreed to aim for a residential library, to raise funds for grants to enable students to do postgraduate degrees in theology and to work towards a Bible dictionary. In 1944 Tyndale House was acquired in Cambridge at a low wartime price. DJ spotted the entire library of a recently deceased Old Testament professor dumped, unclassified, in a second-hand bookshop, and bought the lot as the start of the research library there. John Laing, the builder (later Sir John Laing), was persuaded by DJ to take an interest in these plans, though he would rarely give the total amount needed for any project. Normally he would contribute no more than 50%, and then only if others had first decided that a plan should be pursued. He never tried to direct policy by offering money before a decision was made. It is interesting that not only John Laing, but also F. F. Bruce and W. J. Martin were Brethren.

Lloyd-Jones stressed at this 1941 conference that research ought to be done under the guidance of an overall biblical theology – an ideal that is always hard to maintain.

DJ and Lloyd-Jones

DJ was not a good public speaker, but had a remarkable ability to enthuse and stimulate others. He was always in the background pushing others to take the lead. His huge correspondence, mostly handwritten, witty and often very long, spanned the world and was a constant inspiration to many. He had read both English and medicine at London University and completed the King's College Theology Diploma (AKC) while doing so. He read very widely, was full of fun and cared not at all for what the religious 'brass hats' thought. I once had occasion to tell him that more than half of the St Andrews University Christian Union had departed to join the Student Christian Movement, leaving the CU, now in the hands of what had been called 'people who count for absolutely nothing in the university', to appoint a first year as President. His response was that that sounded more like the church of the book of Acts! He taught others never to be impressed by what 'important' people said or thought, and to be specially wary if they started to flatter one, often quoting Proverbs 29:5: 'Whoever flatters his neighbour is spreading a net for his feet.'

DJ was an inspiring factor in many developments right up to his retiring as IVF General Secretary in 1964, after which he continued to give leadership in the Christian Medical Fellowship for a further ten years. Yet he was always personally inconspicuous and worked with numerous other people. If he was the most important factor in the recovery of a theologically adequate evangelicalism at that time, he would have been the first to protest that others had done more than he had. Nevertheless, he was often the initiator and the tireless correspondent, keeping people in the Forces and elsewhere in touch with developments. He kept the IVF to its proper task, often quoting a maxim of naval strategy: 'First decide what it is that you want to do, and then never take your eyes off that until it is accomplished.' This prevented the IVF from losing its impetus by adopting several worthy tasks that DJ managed to get others to undertake, such as introducing the Fact and Faith films to the UK, and developing the London Bible College, school CUs and hostels for overseas students, even though the IVF was urged to do more in these matters. He always avoided getting into photographs, on at least one occasion locking himself into a lavatory so that he could not be found!

DJ had a close affinity with Dr Lloyd-Jones, though their roles were so different. Both were medical men turned Christian worker, and they became good friends, exchanging book recommendations and sharing in many activities. They were able to help each other, and a letter from Lloyd-Jones to DJ shows that DJ became an important support to the preacher in his times of discouragement. No doubt this was returned. DJ was gifted in the generous friendships he extended to many. He wrote to me almost every week when I was Chairman of the student Executive Committee, forcing me to share in decision making, and he gave books that he thought would help me spiritually. He and Vereker urged Lloyd-Jones to start a quarterly meeting of CEs in lay or ordained ministry. This began in 1941 and still continues, as the Westminster Fellowship, today. It became a very important activity after the war, with membership rising to between 250 and 300, mostly Free Church ministers. As long as Lloyd-Jones chaired it, it was an occasion when sloppy thinking, poor exposition and poor theology were mercilessly demolished. He taught people to think much more in terms of doctrine and of what the Bible does actually say.

Lloyd-Jones had been a distinguished physician at St Bartholomew's (Bart's) Hospital in London. Finding that many of his patients' real problems were more spiritual than medical, in 1926 he resigned and, without further training, started as a minister in a not very large church in South Wales. He soon became a focus of CE work in Wales, but was called back to London in 1938 to be assistant minister to Campbell Morgan at Westminster Chapel. When he followed Campbell Morgan as minister in 1943, he had already become a major force in British evangelicalism.

DJ had to work hard to draw Lloyd-Jones back into the IVF after his first conference in 1935. On that occasion he had been greatly disappointed by the superficiality of the students, though he welcomed their zeal. He was, however, the main speaker at IVF conferences for several years during the war, as well as later. He was President of the IVF for the years 1940–43 and Chairman of their senior Advisory Committee. Lloyd-Jones became a major influence in the movement and once described himself as 'the unofficial theologian of the IVF'. The IVF conferences were growing in size, and he had great influence also at the smaller but important theological students' conferences, which, among other students, included William Still, Gwyn Walters and Elwyn Davies. With Lloyd-Jones speaking, good numbers of Welsh students attended, and he continued through that to have considerable influence on the rising young leaders of CE work in the Principality. At this stage his views on the limits of co-operation were not fixed, and the IVF student Executive Committee remonstrated with their President when he preached at a chaplains' and SCM mission in Oxford with William Temple and a more liberal speaker as other missioners. The student leaders felt that it blurred the distinctions between a CE and a liberal message. As Chairman of the student 'Exec' I had to head a small delegation for this purpose. Lloyd-Jones defended his then current policy of preaching almost wherever he could reach those who rarely heard the gospel.

The wartime IVF conferences were important. When in 1940 the war situation forced a late cancellation of the venue, it was transferred at short notice to Cambridge and met in Trinity College, which had provided the first meal and a lecture room. Rationing created a rather hilarious scramble to feed 150 people in the Guildhall on a diet of vegetable Cornish pasties! Lloyd-Jones gave a memorable Presidential Address on the raising of Jairus's daughter (Lk. 8:41–56). He focused on verse 53: 'They laughed him [Jesus] to scorn, *knowing* that she was dead' (AV), emphasizing the limitations of human knowledge and the power of Christ. The Master of Trinity, the historian G. M. Trevelyan, who was not a believer, attended and greeted Lloyd-Jones at the end with: 'Sir, it has been given to you to speak with great power.' The Professor of Philosophy, C. D. Broad, who was also present, expressed his surprised appreciation that evangelicals could find such speakers.

The ability of the CEs, and particularly DJ, to bring together a strong team of volunteers to work to recapture some of the ground for biblical thinking and a more solid evangelism was to prove very important after the war. CEs were beginning to think much more in terms of doctrine and to love and care for it, not least, as Lloyd-Jones often demonstrated, because you cannot resolve practical and pastoral problems satisfactorily without a doctrinal foundation. Very wisely, in the then atmosphere in CE circles, he insisted that the open discussions at Westminster Chapel must always start not with a theoretical or doctrinal question but with a practical one. Within a short time, however, he had shown that doctrine was essential to solve the practical problems.

Lloyd-Jones also set a pattern in his preaching that was new for many. This had two outstanding features. First, he emphasized the doctrine about, and the character of, God: Father, Son and Holy Spirit. In particular he stressed the doctrine of the Father in a way that was not common in evangelical circles: his holiness, his wisdom, his initiative in our salvation and his power and sovereignty. His preaching was intensely God-centred compared with the rather human-centred emphases that were common then, which had resulted in a stress on what we can *get* in the way of experience or other blessings. It was difficult to come away from the Westminster Chapel services without a fresh sense of awe at the astonishing love of a holy God shown in the gospel.

Yet, as he put it, 'We are not interested in doctrines merely as doctrines, but simply as they bring us to know God.' At the same time, his ministry was essentially Christ-centred. While he held that we must begin with the doctrine of God the Father (as the Old Testament does) he could say: 'The whole essence of the Christian position is dependent on the person of the Lord Jesus Christ . . . Christianity, as has often been pointed out, is Christ Himself. He is not only central, He is absolutely vital . . . we are concerned primarily and always with Him.' His evangelism was often long-term in its impact, though some were converted on first hearing him. He could write: 'I am never tired of saying that the real difficulty of evangelism today is that we do not spend sufficient time with the doctrine of God.'[7] This compares interestingly with John Wesley's urging his preachers to preach the law first, before they came on to the gospel, lest the gospel seem too easy.

Secondly, Lloyd-Jones would work steadily through a Bible book or passage in a way that has become very rare. Most preachers had taken a verse, phrase or topic in isolation. Apart from other advantages, this systematic expository method forced preachers, as Lloyd-Jones himself confessed, to tackle topics they would not otherwise have addressed, and prevented their always returning to their favourite themes. More positively, it meant presenting something nearer to the balance and range of the Bible itself. His expositions were also a model of exposing the doctrinal issues lying behind the particular statements of Scripture. His early sermons (later published) on Philippians and 2 Peter, as well as Old Testament series on Habakkuk and some psalms, give a good idea of the impact that these could make.[8]

Such consecutive preaching also made preachers try to follow the train of thought of the writer, and so to demonstrate more clearly that what they were saying was in fact what the Bible was teaching and not their own fancy imposed upon it. This helped the increasingly well-educated hearers in two respects. It showed them that the Bible had a consistent train of thought from creation to eternity, into which particular verses or themes fitted. It also encouraged them to see that exposition was not just the preserve of those who had been trained to preach. To some extent the method deflated the mystique of the preacher, which some wanted to cultivate, and so aided the development of lay ministry and the renewal of the belief that the Bible can be understood by ordinary people (as the Reformation principle of the perspicuity of Scripture had expressed it). It restrained preachers from saying, 'I tell you that this verse means X', or simply, 'I believe it means X' (let alone 'God has told me that it means X'), since they had to *show* that the Bible actually does say X.

New leaders

Much of the CE leadership was young, partly because there were few older people available, but also because it was the deliberate policy of DJ and others to give responsibility to young and promising people if they were well taught. It has to be confessed that those who were involved sometimes blush at the memory of things they said and did. They were rarely polished advocates of the cause. God, nevertheless, was pleased to bless what was done, and again and again the strength of a biblical message asserted itself.

A good many future leaders of CE churches and causes, and some notable missionaries such as Helen Roseveare and Ruth Watson, were CU leaders in the 1940s.[9] This has been particularly well documented in Wales.[10] The small CUs there were seeing the conversion of a fair number, and the establishment of others who were to become the future leaders of the Evangelical Movement of Wales, and ministers, or wives of the ministers, of some of the largest congregations in the Principality.

Another significant feature of these developments is the style of leadership. Lloyd-Jones, Stibbs, Manley and Guillebaud were basically shy men who did not seek the limelight. Lloyd-Jones used to say that when he and Stibbs were together at a conference, they both found it difficult to mix in, and were soon to be found quietly drinking coffee together in a corner. None of the leaders of what proved to be a major renewal of evangelical strength were examples of the strong leadership frequently advocated in business or management today. If they were expounding the Bible, it was a different matter, as they spoke with the authority of the Bible message. Stibbs's expositions were often memorable, especially his communion addresses, though he was never so good on paper. These men were not naturally forceful leaders, but their leadership was mightily effective.

C. S. Lewis and others

Radio was by now very important (television at that stage was limited to one channel available to those in the London area who could afford a set). Almost everyone wanted to listen, at least to the radio news of the war. When C. S. Lewis started giving radio talks in 1941, he had a very wide audience. He did not have an impressive presence as a public speaker, but these talks made considerable impact, and when they were published as *Broadcast Talks* (1942),

Christian Behaviour (1943) and *Beyond Personality* (1944) they began to circulate extensively.[11] His writings had a very wide influence, well beyond evangelical circles. His book *The Problem of Pain* had appeared in 1940 (and was reprinted six times in 1940 and 1941 alone). *The Abolition of Man* (1943) was a particular reproof to liberalism. Lewis was never an evangelical, but he made traditional orthodoxy both attractive and convincing. Evangelicals used his books enthusiastically, and he gave them and others a fresh confidence that it was possible to proclaim orthodox beliefs as intellectually defensible in the face of attacks from any quarter. It had been common for evangelicals to appeal largely to experience, but they were helped by Lewis and others to be bolder in apologetics and in a much more doctrinal approach.

Lewis had another effect. The lines between CEs and others had been so tightly drawn that CEs had found it hard to see any good in what did not come out of their own circle. Now they found that there was valuable material coming from other sources which they could use effectively in the right context. The same thing was brought home to many who were in the Forces, including some of the chaplains, when they were obliged to work with those of other traditions. Without altering their own stances, they discovered that some of the high-church party, particularly, were more spiritually minded and more orthodox than they had realized, and they learned to respect their position. This helped evangelicals, and especially the CEs, to read more widely and to have better relations with others. In any case, there was not an enormous amount of CE literature of good quality available. IVF books were being more widely read. T. C. Hammond's *Perfect Freedom* (1938) was an introduction to ethics, and his *Reasoning Faith*, an introduction to apologetics, appeared in 1943. Clearly the number of authors suitable for the IVF was not large! Paper rationing meant that it was not easy even to reprint all the books, let alone produce many new ones.

The influence of Karl Barth became important during these years, especially in Presbyterian circles. It was never great in Anglican, Methodist or Baptist circles, but it did weaken the hold of liberalism. Barth's *The Epistle to the Romans* appeared in German in 1919, and E. C. Hoskyns had published an English translation in 1932. G. T. Thomson (Professor of Dogmatics at Edinburgh, 1936–52) had published a translation of the first part of the *Church Dogmatics* in 1936. Barth's influence, however, did not really grow in the UK until the 1940s and 1950s. Tom Torrance, who had been a leader in the IVF's work among theological students, studied under Barth in Switzerland and became a spokesman for Barth's theology upon becoming Professor at

Edinburgh in 1952.[12] The reaction of evangelicals was mixed. Unlike Torrance and G. T. Thomson, many who came into Barthianism from a liberal background retained an advanced critical position on the Bible, which put off CEs. It was, however, a move towards accepting divine revelation as the basis of all theology, and so was a further blow to liberalism. It was Christ-centred and not human-centred, as so much theology had become. It attracted vigorous criticism from many quarters, but was a breath of fresh air and helped to undermine to some extent the liberal consensus of the university faculties of theology. Most CEs were not able to accept it because it did not seem to them to rest clearly enough on biblical exposition, and allowed its adherents to doubt the reliability of the Bible.

Max Warren, who was Secretary of the Church Missionary Society from 1940 to 1963, started the Evangelical Fellowship for Theological Literature in 1942. In this, as in some of his other activities, he hoped to create a middle ground to unite all evangelicals. The membership was mainly LE, though a few prominent CEs joined at first. Several of its members later became theological professors or bishops, but they mostly moved away from a clear evangelical stance and in some cases became quite radically unorthodox. The IVF's Biblical Research Committee inaugurated the annual Tyndale Lectures in 1942 and launched the Tyndale Fellowship for Biblical Research in 1945. These continue in the 1990s and have proved longer-lasting than the EFTL, which was closed in 1972. The general movement of leading LEs towards increasingly unorthodox positions, which EFTL members represented, was beginning to dissolve the LE organizations. The emphasis of Tyndale House and the Tyndale Fellowship was decisively on biblical studies: Old Testament, New Testament and biblical archaeology. The Brethren, who took a leading part in much of it, were experts in these areas, and argued that in any case biblical studies are (or should be) fundamental to all else. The Biblical Theology Group of the TF, chaired by Lloyd-Jones, never attracted the same scholarly people – partly perhaps because there were very few chairs and lectureships in doctrine (except in Scotland), whereas there were good opportunities in the other biblical fields. The resulting weakness in doctrinal areas at a scholarly level was to surface later.

Social trends and wider influence

Society generally was drifting away from its Christian roots towards the outlook of secular humanism. People in all parts of the churches were alarmed by the trend, and Parliament passed R. A. Butler's Education Act in 1944 in response. This required all schools to give religious instruction, and to start the school day with an act of 'collective worship'. Schools were charged 'to contribute towards the spiritual, moral, mental and physical development' of children. This presented an increased opportunity for Christians to teach religious education, but the task often fell to those of an unorthodox position or of no personal faith at all. Children from evangelical churches began to face in the classroom views from which they had previously been protected. In 1947, the school-leaving age was raised to fifteen, extending the impact of secondary education.

Meanwhile, Christians in the professions were facing a breakdown of the formerly accepted standards and morality. Majority apologetic questions were arising, and, inspired again by DJ, there was a growth of professional groups associated with the IVF. In 1940 the IVF launched its Graduates' Fellowship (GF), with representatives from some of the main professions on the committee. The medical section, with DJ as Secretary and Lloyd-Jones as chairman of its 'think-tank', grew rapidly into the Christian Medical Fellowship in 1949, absorbing then the older (and elderly) Medical Prayer Union. At DJ's suggestion, and with myself as a PhD student as Secretary, the Research Scientists' Christian Fellowship (now Christians in Science) held its first conference in 1944, with a dozen research students and just two university teachers. The schoolteachers' group, which had been started before the war, worked on the production of books and other literature. A Graduates' Fellowship newsletter began in 1940, with an article by Lloyd-Jones urging readers to seize the opportunities of wartime for bold witness. The newsletter was planned partly to keep in touch with members in the Forces, but grew in 1949 into *The Christian Graduate* magazine, which was to be important for the next four decades, reaching a circulation of over 11,000 at its peak. One of the stated aims of the GF was 'to endeavour to lead the way in securing a more adequate and scholarly evangelical literature'. If it seems strange that the IVF should have been looked to as the leader in these areas, it must be remembered that the universities were, much more than today, a unique resource for intellectual effort and the forming of opinion. The media were far less important than today, and in any case evangelicals had little access to them.

John Stott, who was to exert such a remarkable influence later, was a theological student in Cambridge during the war. He faced many of the problems of someone coming from a more pietistic background. He had been converted as a schoolboy through E. J. H. Nash ('Bash'), and was taught and trained by Bash to be his right-hand man. Nevertheless, he found himself poorly equipped to deal with liberal theology. Derek Kidner, who was the CICCU President in 1942–3, had set an important example in tackling theology with seriousness and integrity, getting a first and going on to be an important author. Many others professed to have got through the course largely by ignoring its content, sometimes claiming to have spent lectures reading the daily paper. John Stott had the same ideal as Kidner, and, after a degree in languages, launched into theology. He struggled quite acutely at times, though he came out of it with his faith undimmed. He commented later, 'I sometimes wonder on which particular scrapheap I would be today, if it had not been for God's providential gift of the UCCF.'[13]

Student numbers were greatly reduced in the war years, and CUs were still small as a rule. They were, however, seeing conversions on a scale that was new, not often in total numbers, but in relation to their size. When, for example, the Sheffield CU was reduced to six members, two of their friends were converted, so that there were eight before the end of the year. CU members prayed earnestly for the weaker CUs. A great appeal for prayer was made at one conference for St Andrews University, where there were only four members; there was rejoicing the following year to hear that there were thirty. Young CEs were beginning to find a warm fellowship in battling for what they believed was a true gospel witness of a kind that had been eclipsed. Throughout the country there was a sense of confidently fighting together for the truth.

The IVF took its work into the teacher training colleges. A small start had been made in 1935, and now regular conferences for such colleges grew in size. At the 1944 conference, plans were laid for similar efforts in the technical, art and agricultural colleges with Eric Richardson (now Sir Eric Richardson) as chairman. He owed much to the National Young Life Campaign, and had been President of the Liverpool University CU when an attempted takeover by the Oxford Group had to be resisted.[14] By 1944 he was principal of a technical college and soon after became principal of the premier technical college in Britain, the Regent Street Polytechnic (now the University of Westminster). For many years he helped to steer this work as the colleges were gradually upgraded, first to colleges of advanced technology, then polytechnics, and now universities. At this stage, however, college students were often younger and less academic than in universities, and the type of witness needed was different. This led the IVF to appoint separate staff and, to a limited extent, to produce different literature. The SCM did not attempt to work in the 'techs', and a liberal Christianity could hardly survive there anyway. Both the college sections of IVF produced some fine missionaries after the war.

The British Council of Churches was created in 1942, and plans were laid for the World Council of Churches to be formed when the war was over. Evangelicals were divided over their attitude to this ecumenism; few were particularly enthusiastic, and many CEs were deeply suspicious as to where it would lead. They were happy to co-operate with other CEs across denominational boundaries in interdenominational organizations, though at a local level there was hardly any joint activity, denominational boundaries still being strong.

Bible study

A development that attracted little attention at the time was the production by the IVF of a new kind of Bible study material for groups. It had been the custom for Bible teaching in the student world, and the midweek meetings of churches, to be in the form of an exposition by a minister or other speaker. This was, as a rule, a sort of mini-Keswick address: Bible-based, but requiring of the attenders only a passive role. As the CUs increased in size, and as halls of residence multiplied, each with its own Bible-study group, there were not enough people to take these meetings in the student world. G. T. Manley, who had experience of missionary study groups in churches, proposed discussion-type studies that could be led by less professional people. The IVF produced study outlines with suggested questions, and these quickly became the norm for such student groups and were taken up in many churches. One of their several advantages was that they helped everyone to articulate their faith and forced them to work out for themselves what a passage meant. As the King James Version was in universal use, usually without any paragraphs or sub-headings, the first task was to try to find the train of thought in what one young person described as 'a string of apparently disconnected verses'.

The IVF spent a good deal of energy in training leaders, and they were often foremost in introducing such studies into the churches so that small groups could be developed there, sometimes in congregations of a very different tradition. This was more important than it might now seem, because ministers of all traditions (including CEs) were very slow to encourage anyone who was not ordained to preach or teach in the church context. The new method removed any danger of a supine acceptance of human authorities, and helped those concerned to try to make sure that what came out of the study was what was really there in the passage. Leadership of a group was often the first step to a more responsible role.

1945

There were sad casualties of war in all sections of the churches, though they were not anything like as severe as in the First World War. What altered the situation more than the casualties was the weeding-out effect on those whose faith was not tough enough to stand the pressures. Those with strong roots in the Bible seemed to come out of it best, and that was true in all sections of the churches. The Officers' Christian Union, and the corresponding organizations for 'other ranks', did excellent work. It is not insignificant that while these bodies did not have strong doctrinal tests, and were open to all, they were overwhelmingly CE in emphasis, because few others had the stamina for such witness in wartime. This weeding-out process was to spread to the tougher areas of life after the war, so that LE and liberal organizations crumbled and were replaced increasingly by those of a CE colour as society became more and more secularized.

By the end of the war CEs were in a new situation, though it was not noticed by others. They were more confident, less defensive, more widely aware of the thinking of others and more forward-looking. Above all, they were better able to think in terms of doctrine and to defend and preach accordingly. They were hoping to recapture ground and were in at least some cases concerned to think more searchingly about what it means to be a Christian in the world. They had a young and reasonably competent up-and-coming educated element able to cope with apologetics and evangelism at the student level, even if not at a more learned level. CEs were all set for advance. It may have seemed a sign no larger than 'a cloud as small as a man's hand', and their leadership was 'no better than their fathers', but the movement had considerable promise of future growth, because CEs were better equipped doctrinally. Hence they could grapple with the thinking of non-Christians and see how to apply the faith in every area.

Another important lesson from the war was that a simple pietistic faith, fed by constant reading of the Bible, was well able to meet the anxieties and tragedies of the times. This was as true for those at home subject to bombing and bereavements as to those actually in the Forces. One student told me that since his recent evangelical conversion, he was now able confidently to face the possibility of being killed by a bomb the next night, something he could not have said before, in spite of a very religious training. As society became more and more hostile to a Christian position in the next decades, it emerged that this was true in other tough areas of life. A biblical faith was uniquely able to stand up, while other varieties of belief failed increasingly, when the pressures of life intensified.

4. NEW BEGINNINGS
1945–55

No-one was sure what would emerge from the devastation of the war. Demobilization was fairly rapid, but national service continued until 1963 and rationing was relaxed only gradually. Only slowly could churches return to a more normal pattern. These years, however, saw a number of very significant changes.

New promise in the churches

In 1945 John Stott was ordained and became curate at All Souls Church, Langham Place, London (he became rector in 1950). In the same year, William Still started his ministry at Gilcomston South Church, Aberdeen. Both ministries were to prove of enormous importance, and Still began systematic preaching through Bible books or passages.

In *Ireland* in the same year, Herbert Carson was ordained to the Church of Ireland ministry. He had gathered a group of like-minded theological students at Trinity College, Dublin, during his course there, and had considerable influence from 1948 to 1952 as the only (part-time) IVF travelling secretary for Ireland and part of Northern England, while he was also the CSSM (now Scripture Union) worker for school CUs. The CU at Trinity, where all Church of Ireland ordinands had to train, was producing some fine future leaders, several of whom went abroad as missionaries. They were greatly helped by the Professor of Physiology, David Torrens. Anglican clergy looked informally for advice to an older parson, J. C. Robb, who, having gone prematurely blind, was generous in fellowship and friendship. The Ruanda Mission and BCMS provided some fellowship. Northern Ireland was strikingly more religious and church-going than the rest of Britain. In 1968–9 a survey found that only 2% of people in Northern Ireland declared that they were 'not members of a church, faith or religion' compared with nearly 25% in England, Scotland and Wales.[1] When in this period an IVF conference had a discussion on the question 'Do Moody's methods work today?' it was only the Irish students who voted enthusiastically 'Yes'. There had been some remarkable evangelistic moves during the war in Northern Ireland, including something of a revival in the main college of education, Stranmillis, while the CU was forbidden to hold meetings of more than three people.

The most important evangelical in Ireland in this period was almost certainly T. S. Mooney, a bank manager in Londonderry.[2] Almost half of the Presbyterian ministerial students had to pass through Magee College in Londonderry in those days. He befriended them, fed them extremely well in his bachelor lodgings, took them to the large Crusader class that he ran, and above all lent them books and discussed their courses, and so saved them from the liberal influences that few of them were equipped to withstand on their own. He was not a graduate, but knew which books would help his student friends. In speaking at a public meeting for the IVF, he once started by saying that he thought he was well qualified to talk about the universities because he had once spent a weekend in Cambridge and had passed through Oxford in the train! In fact, he was deadly serious underneath the humour, and taught many to trust and love the Bible whatever the authorities might say. An extraordinary number of leading CE lay people all over Britain today are products of his Crusader class and his personal friendship. His influence still spreads far and wide into several denominations.

In *Scotland* the Church of Scotland was, and still is, overwhelmingly the largest Protestant church and has always been more homogeneous than the Anglican churches. It never had parties within it in the twentieth century, and those who called themselves evangelical (in a few cases LE, as before the war) were active in all sorts of denominational affairs. Interdenominational missionary societies and conventions of a Keswick type continued to be influential, but there was a flurry of evangelistic activity from all the churches. D. P. Thomson for the Church of Scotland Home Board encouraged team missions, and 'Tell Scotland', led by Tom Allan, peaked in 1955 with the Kelvin Hall Crusade in Glasgow. There were only one or two theological teachers who could have been called CE, but Barthianism began to provide a theologically competent alternative to liberalism.

In *Wales* in July 1945 a remarkable student-led mission in Llanelli launched a new evangelical thrust in the Principality, which gave the student team a new certainty that the old gospel was still as much as ever the power of God. Martyn Lloyd-Jones was at first hesitant about this student-led thrust, but gave his advice and friendship to the leaders, whom he met, usually, at the IVF conferences in England, which he and they attended. A number of future ministers were converted while they were theological students, including Vernon Higham, Derek Swann and Eryl Davies. The Llanelli mission had set another future leader, Elwyn Davies, an unconverted theological student at the time, on a path that led to his conversion in 1947. He became a leader among Welsh-speaking students in Bangor.

In 1948, the Welsh-language magazine *Y Cylchgrawn Efengylaid* (*The Evangelical Magazine*) was launched, and the teams running town missions had an evangelistic presence at the National Eisteddfod which included by no means only students. People spoke of 'the people of the Magazine'. In 1954, camps for schoolchildren in both Welsh and English were started. The Evangelical Movement of Wales (1955) grew out of these essentially grass-roots activities.[3] Strongly evangelical ministries became more numerous in Wales, notably the ministry of Emrys Davies at Mount Pleasant Baptist Church in the centre of Swansea, with monthly rallies of over a thousand young people and the encouragement and equipment of many for future service.[4]

Lloyd-Jones repeatedly emphasized the necessity of a more doctrinal and thoughtful Christianity, which he and John Stott and other younger preachers exemplified. The intellectual inferiority complex faded, not because these people had great intellects (though they were competent and very sharp thinkers), but because, as these humble people of God showed, the Bible properly preached was more than equal to all its rivals. I do not think that anyone accused these new leaders of being self-confident.

In *England* CE Methodism focused round Cliff College, though students for the ministry had to complete their training at one of the much more liberal colleges. The Church of England report *Towards the Conversion of England*[5] was published early in 1945 and there were high hopes in some quarters that this would stimulate a new wave of evangelistic activity. The commission that prepared it had been chaired by Bishop Christopher Chavasse. It never caught on, however. It was debated in the Church Assembly before any ex-service people could be there, and the churches were still in a state of recovery, quite apart from the question of how many people were sufficiently sure of their message and well motivated. Chavasse did not have the complete confidence of the CEs, though he was very anxious to draw them into united evangelical efforts. At a more popular level, Tom Rees, who had conducted a number of evangelistic missions during the war, including a number in Northern Ireland and Dublin, now ran fifty-four mass rallies in the Albert Hall, London, with many, especially young people, professing conversion. There was a rapid development of fruitful evangelistic activities of all sorts.

Ex-service personnel and literature

A major new factor in this was the return of war-toughened Christians into the life of the churches. A great many of these had learned to draw their strength from a prayerful reading of the Bible when there were few other supports. The teachers in the theological colleges and faculties and in training institutes for religious education, who had mostly not been in the Forces, were still churning out what they had learned in the 1920s and 1930s. The students, however, had changed. There was a clash in some colleges between the staff and the older, experienced students who knew more of life than their tutors. Some of the evangelical students would not so easily accept what they were being taught, and wanted to meet separately for prayer and discussion. That upset the staff because it 'threatened the unity of the college'. Questions after lectures became sharper and more difficult for staff to answer. A steady trickle of convinced CE students began to come out of the colleges and faculties into the ministry. This included Sidney Lawrence in Methodism and Stanley Voke among the Baptists.

The IVF's Theological Students Fellowship (now the Religious and Theological Studies Fellowship) was growing. Its annual conference, usually with either Lloyd-Jones or J. I. Packer playing an important part, had considerable influence. The Fellowship was not, however, large. Eric Alexander reports that when he was a student in Glasgow (1954–7), a caustic student chairman announced that the TSF group would meet after dinner in the telephone box. Unfortunately, that would have been almost possible. The TSF helped many, though there was still very little up-to-date literature available to support them. Its members looked to the conferences, to a few leaders and to some small theological monographs published by the IVF. These were a great encouragement because they showed that conservative scholarship could hold its own in at least some important areas.

In 1947 the IVF published its *New Bible Handbook*, edited by G. T. Manley. It sold out within a few weeks. It was not until 1953 that they published the *New Bible Commentary*. There had been no one-volume commentary for a long time, and for the IVF it was a big venture. Its immediate success meant that it gave an unexpected financial boost to the IVF's publishing programme, enabling them to be more ambitious and to start on the Tyndale Commentaries and other projects. It was, however, decided to publish some titles under a different imprint – Tyndale Press – because it was said that lecturers could not bring themselves to recommend anything with the name 'IVF' attached to it! At one of the most prestigious departments for religious education, in London, a librarian reported that the head of the department had requested that IVF books, including the *New Bible Commentary*, be removed to stacks where they were very difficult to access. Having lunch one day at London Bible College, I rather mischievously asked the Principal (E. F. Kevan) whether liberal books were available to his students in the library. He replied that they certainly were, because his students needed to know what others were thinking. The illiberalism of the liberals was much in evidence, and compared badly with a place like London Bible College.

Ronald Inchley returned from wartime service to be IVF's Publications Secretary in 1945, and did a truly remarkable job until he retired in 1977. He was another who kept a low profile personally, but he became an admired leader in the world of evangelical literature. He launched a series of new authors, including J. I. Packer, Michael Griffiths, Michael Green, John Wenham, Donald Guthrie and Francis Schaeffer. The IVF's publishing programme (only in 1968 was the name Inter-Varsity Press adopted) became in the minds of many a standard-bearer for classical evangelicalism and its influence quickly spread worldwide. The *New Bible Commentary*, for instance, was translated into several languages. In Japanese it provided the only commentary in print on some books of the Bible, and the initial edition sold out in a few months. IVP's editorial policy had always been very positively proactive, and 'RI' used sometimes to take possible authors out for country walks to plan new books.

The student world

Student numbers grew rapidly, including many ex-service men and women. Opposition to evangelical witness was still strong. Probably the fiercest battles were in the teacher training colleges, which were then mostly residential institutions devoted entirely to education, many of them Church of England foundations. The SCM had been strong here, and the idea that a separate, distinctively evangelical group should exist was anathema to the staff. The first RE lecture of the course was liable to include a request that all those who believed in the reliability of the Bible should raise their hands so that they could be subjected to vigorous attack by the lecturer, frequently including some ridicule. In this way it was apparently thought that they would be better teachers of Christianity than if they had received a stirring treatment of the deity and majesty of Christ. Meanwhile the staff turned a blind eye to near-blasphemous goings on in the initiation programmes run by the students.[6] That so many survived this treatment was a bafflement to the staff, who were sometimes angry that students became more conservative as the course proceeded, through the influence of the CU. One college principal, who told a student trying to start a CU that she would be tightly controlled from the IVF, replied in astonishment: 'But how? There is only Ros, isn't there?' Rosalyn Carrick was the Secretary for the training colleges. Lecturers found it incredible that students should hold such strong convictions simply as a result of reading the Bible and in the face of the liberal teaching that they were receiving. Lily Sayers (née Picket) relates how, even at Homerton College in Cambridge in the 1933–5 period, their small CU was not at first allowed to put up notices of meetings, and was constantly harried by lecturers and criticized for finding help in the university CU and a local church.[7]

The IVF ran separate conferences for these colleges, and appointed staff with experience of them as well as getting the help of teachers on a spare-time basis. Interestingly, one critical college principal, who quizzed the CU leaders on what they did, acknowledged that the discussion type of Bible study that they were using was educationally rather good. Mistakes were made, however, in the heat of the battle. Students sometimes cast doubt on the reality of the faith of the staff, and long-time church members found this intolerable (though their apparent hostility to orthodox Christian belief had provoked such a response). CU members had to prove themselves by better work in RE, and the pressure gradually subsided as the SCM weakened and the IVF arranged for public questions to be asked in the Church of England Assembly as to why Bible study groups were being discouraged in the Anglican colleges. What was happening in the colleges reflected the situation in many schools and churches.

The universities were expanding, and technical colleges grew in academic level and student numbers. In the latter, where there was hardly any Christian witness, the IVF grew apace. In the universities the SCM began to falter, though it still had much official support. It was further weakened by the growth of denominational societies supported by chaplaincies, particularly the Methodist societies. This also meant that not so many Methodists joined the CUs; as a result, there were fewer CE Methodist leaders in the 1960s and

1970s than in most other denominations. There were, of course, exceptions. Donald English, who had been converted in his first year at Leicester University and was an IVF travelling secretary from 1955 to 1958, rose eventually to being twice elected as President of the Conference – an honour unique since 1932.

Grants for tertiary studies became much more widely available. Denominations that had rarely encouraged their young people to go to university, such as the Salvation Army and most Baptist churches, began to do so. As a result, the influence of the Brethren in the IVF was diluted, though not reduced in numbers. The IVF's CUs grew quickly and had some very experienced leaders. Leon Dale, the CU President in London, had been a colonel in the Artillery,[8] and the Oxford President, Donald Wiseman, had been a group captain in the RAF in the Italy campaign. He was to become Professor of Assyriology in the University of London, and a prolific writer and speaker on Old Testament-related topics. The CUs carried out large-scale university missions which reached a high proportion of the student body (certainly up to 50% in some cases), and resulted in a considerable number of conversions, often in the weeks or months after the mission when people had had time to think it over.

John Stott and Leith Samuel emerged as outstanding university missioners. John Stott led missions in Cambridge in 1952 and 1958, and in Oxford in 1954 and 1957, as well as in Durham and other centres. In these places there were many future Anglican ministers. People in the liberal and high-church traditions commented that Stott seemed to represent a new kind of evangelicalism that was intellectually adequate for the universities. Leith Samuel concentrated on the modern universities, where his answering of questions after the addresses gave a fresh model to many. The example of these and other preachers gave a vision for the ministry, and a growing number of evangelicals offered and began to train. Some of these had been recently converted as students, such as David Watson, who became an outstanding evangelist. CU members became bold and more competent in personal evangelism.

The leaders were preachers rather than theologians, and the whole growing movement had all the signs of being a fresh discovery of biblical truth by innumerable ordinary people. One student at London Bible College said he thought he had learned more about how to think doctrinally by sitting in the gallery at Westminster Chapel on Sundays than in all his theological studies. John Stott's book *Basic Christianity* (1958) was based on his mission addresses, and it not only provided a tool for evangelism but also helped to give many a fresh view of revealed truth as a unity at a basic level.[9] The book has had a huge circulation worldwide and has been translated into fifty languages. This view of the coherence of revealed truth and its grandeur as a consistent whole, which T. C. Hammond's *In Understanding be Men* had given to many, captured the enthusiasm of people in a way that particular truths had rarely done. The considerable reading that DJ required of the staff for their summer staff conference was an education! The ordained staff benefited as much as the others, as their theological training had usually contained very little doctrine or apologetics.

Although the ex-service men and women included some strong leaders, they were not always theologically discerning, and the IVF continued to have a battle to keep its witness clear at the local CU level. This creative conflict, however, trained up some leaders who were to have an important role in the next decades. Similar issues arose in local churches over how clear their doctrinal stand was to be.

At the same time, evangelical apologetics improved greatly. The evangelistic programmes and missions in the student world contained a good deal of apologetics, as well as meetings for different faculties, which used a Christian approach to academic subjects as a way of winning attention to the gospel.

Donald MacKay emerged as an outstanding lecturer who was brilliant in answering questions.[10] He was at that time a lecturer in physics at King's College, London, and later exercised a long ministry in this area as Professor of Communication at Keele University. Among other important contributions, MacKay answered those who talked of 'Nature' as just a machine, not by looking for things that could not be explained in those terms, but by stressing God's sovereignty in all events whether we could 'explain' them or not. Much evangelical apologetics had unwisely accepted what was really a deistic view of nature as a mechanism set up by God at the start but now operating 'on its own'. Miracles were then accepted as breaches of natural law or what is scientifically impossible (the agnostics' definition). In relation to nature this reduced God to 'the God of the gaps'. Unfortunately, C. S. Lewis, in his weakest but influential book *Miracles*, seemed to reinforce such a position. MacKay helped people to a more biblical view of God as Creator and '*Upholder* of all things', which had been largely lost sight of in CE circles. In this approach the processes of nature are just as much a cause of awe and praise to God as are the events that we cannot explain in scientific terms. It was no longer necessary to seek out inexplicable phenomena as evidences for the existence of God. MacKay had much more to his ministry, but this aspect, which arose out of the biblical doctrine of God, was an example of how the recovery of doctrine strengthened the CE cause. If this emphasis is largely taken for granted today, that shows how influential it was.

Norman Anderson found a wide-ranging ministry, first as Warden of Tyndale House and then as a lecturer and professor of law in London. His Bible expositions were a model, and his small booklet *The Evidence for the Resurrection*, based on his talks and published by the IVF in 1950, was very widely used and reached a circulation of 215,000 by 1997. A number of other less notable speakers also tackled apologetic themes. The CUs and the churches found that lectures of an apologetic nature on science and faith or other topical interests did break new ground with non-Christians and led to their giving fresh attention to the gospel. In any case, Christians were expected to be able to give a good answer to the questions raised by their friends, and wanted help in doing so. The IVF was being looked to increasingly as the standard-bearer of the resurgent evangelicalism. One of the leading Brethren preachers remarked that, while he thought that Brethrenism had been raised up by God to keep the gospel alive during a time when it was little heard in the mixed denominations, that task was now being given in considerable measure also to the IVF.[11] The CE positions were well defined doctrinally, frequently around the basic truths that were conveniently expressed in the IVF's eight-point Doctrinal Basis,[12] which new churches and other organizations often adopted as their own. Churches found a new, vigorous, lay leadership, and the number of CE churches increased steadily.

This was particularly notable in Wales. In 1949 the IVF appointed its first Welsh travelling secretary. This was Gwyn Walters, a bilingual theologian with a PhD from Edinburgh. He had an effective ministry in evangelism and in defending biblical orthodoxy. He had been converted through the Cardiff CU in 1940, and obtained his release from the Presbyterian Church of Wales only with considerable difficulty and through the intervention of Ieuan Phillips, after people had protested about letting him help such a body as the IVF.[13] Lloyd-Jones spoke at the Welsh IVF conferences in 1950 and 1952, and then refused invitations to return, as he believed they were well launched. In 1953 the Evangelical Movement of Wales was started, and in 1955 Elwyn Davies became its first half-time Secretary as well as a half-time travelling secretary for the Welsh IVF. In 1955 Lloyd-Jones returned for the first Welsh ministers' conference and, although he refused to become an active force in the Welsh work, he had largely moulded the theological emphases towards a decidedly Reformed view. This has been a mark of most, but not all, Welsh evangelicalism up to the present. The EMW was to become the major evangelical force in Wales, developing theological training, literature, camps and conferences that have grown steadily to the present day.

The IVF had been pressed to affiliate school CUs, but had not felt that it could take that on with their limited staff. DJ then persuaded the CSSM (SU) and the two Crusaders' Unions to join with the IVF in sponsoring the Inter-School Christian Fellowship, which CSSM rightly took under their wing and made a major part of their work for the next period in Scotland as well as in England. Branse Burbridge, who had a DFC and bar and DSO and bar, won as a night fighter pilot, became one of their best speakers, with great appeal to the young. The ISCF work in the expanding secondary schools sent up a growing number of well-thought-out people into the churches and the student world.[14] Some well-known wartime leaders, such as General Sir William Dobbie, spoke to large audiences with a simple gospel message.[15]

It was an exhilarating time to be involved in the ISCF and IVF, as CUs grew in size and number and the evangelistic work proved very effective. A high proportion of the student body could be reached in missions. In some CUs a third or even nearly half of their members were people who had come to faith since arriving at university or college, and there was prayer that such fruitfulness would soon be seen in the churches, where, with some exceptions, life was more difficult.

Encouragement in the churches

Evangelical ministers often had a lonely and discouraging time still. Mark Ruston, a former 'Bash Camper' who had taken theology seriously as a student, commented that after seeing a fruitful work in the CU it was depressing to go as a curate into a parish where nothing much seemed to be happening. Ruston was a rather quiet bachelor, an unobtrusive and almost retiring leader, a godly pastor and a man of prayer. A good but not remarkable preacher, he exercised a remarkable ministry as Vicar of the Round Church in the centre of Cambridge from 1955 to 1987. Here he exerted a great influence among students, many of whom sought him out for help and advice.

Encouragement soon arrived in the churches. By 1955, Westminster Chapel and All Souls in London, and Gilcomston South Church in Aberdeen, had become influential models for renewed evangelical church life and expository preaching.

In 1947 the Congregational Revival Fellowship was formed, and in 1952 the Methodist Revival Fellowship, to strengthen the hands of evangelicals in their denominations. In the latter, Sidney Lawrence and Roland Lamb were leaders until they both left Methodism for independent churches. The Baptist Revival Fellowship held its first conference in 1954. The Westminster Fellowship grew in importance, mainly in the Free Churches. In the Church of England, John Stott started the Eclectics in 1955; this was a fellowship of younger clergy (aged under forty) organized in local groups all over England for discussion, prayer and mutual help. Its only rule was the final authority of Scripture. William Still began to provide a link between evangelical ministers in the Church of Scotland. Even if none of these bodies included everyone of like mind, they did help to support and encourage. Evangelical ministers in Ireland formed informal links. The considerable body of over twenty young assistant missioners on university missions helped to provide a sense of belonging to a lively and effective movement in the churches. David Bebbington states that 'Probably the most important factor behind the advance of conservative Evangelicalism in the postwar period was the Inter-Varsity Fellowship'.[16] The informal and largely ministerial fellowships were, however, crucial for many at the next stage of their ministry to encourage and strengthen CEs in their desire to remain faithful to Bible truth and effective evangelism. They still felt themselves to be a rather despised minority in their churches, and before this time many had lost heart or drifted away from a CE position under pressure. Now they knew that they were part of a lively fellowship. DJ wrote at this time that there seemed to be 'a turning of the tide'.

Billy Graham

Since its foundation in 1846, the Evangelical Alliance had tried to bring evangelicals together for united witness. This took on a new importance when in 1954 it organized the massive Billy Graham campaign in the Harringay Arena in London. It was extremely successful, far more so than most people had dared to hope. It was widely supported by evangelical churches, only the more strongly Reformed wing being very hesitant, partly because of their doubts about 'campaign evangelism' in general and also because of the style of the call for decisions. Lloyd-Jones did not identify himself with it, though he did not speak against. A very considerable number of people professed faith and continued as regular church attenders, including not a few who entered the ministry later. It did not bring revival, but it raised the public profile of CE beliefs and made it easier to get a good hearing for the gospel. Perhaps as important was the effect on some of those ministers who had been battered by their theological training. Billy Graham's repeated 'The Bible says', which offended the liberals, gave fresh confidence to preach a straight message from the Bible. Raymond Turvey, who was to prove important later, was far from alone in confessing that he had only now been able to shake off the effects of his liberal theological training through being involved in this campaign.

On one of the Sundays which Graham had free, the appointed preacher for the CICCU service was Fred Crittenden, the IVF Graduates' Secretary and overseas students' worker. He offered to stand down if Graham would take his place. They had tea together before the service, and Crittenden urged Graham not to try to give an apologetic address (as in fact he intended), but to preach in the same way as he would to anyone else. Graham changed his sermon, and from then on continued to preach to students in the ways for which he was most gifted. That policy was to have repercussions later.

Graham's All Scotland Crusade in 1955 in Glasgow had a very significant effect on Scottish church life. Tom Allan, who among a good many others in Scotland had at first been sceptical about mass evangelism, threw his weight wholeheartedly into it. It created some division, but membership of the Church of Scotland peaked soon after, and attendance at Glasgow churches was up by 10,000 the following year. Sales of Bibles soared and the readership of Scripture Union daily Bible reading notes increased by 120,000 in Scotland.[17] Graham reached all classes of society in Scotland as in England, and helped to make classical evangelicalism more acceptable.

Ian Randall, writing from a Baptist perspective, sees the impact of Graham as parallel in the popular sphere to the influence of John Stott and others at a more academic level. He also notes the renewed confidence of evangelicals in general, and specially in evangelism and the straightforward preaching that followed in many circles. 'The change of mood in British evangelicals owes a great deal to . . . Billy Graham',[18] he writes. John Stott and Billy Graham both promoted a fresh vision for a preaching ministry and so, indirectly, increased the number of CEs offering for the ministry.

The Graham campaign had some other surprising effects in view of his very conservative background. His wife Ruth, it was noted, used some make-up! This concerned some of the most conservative, but helped people to see that such things were not really important. The rather legalistic emphasis on such details was weakened because Graham was becoming for many a model of evangelicalism.

Graham also followed a wider policy than had been accepted in inviting people who were certainly not evangelicals to appear on his platform. This again not only upset some supporters but started a dangerous and, in the long run, damaging tradition of using people of status in the churches to give their names or to take the chair at evangelical activities, even if they did not fully support the doctrinal position of the body concerned. Anglicans in particular started appointing bishops of uncertain theology to be chairmen of conferences or patronage trusts, for instance, provided they were generally friendly to what was being done. The later Graham crusades ran into some real difficulties over this, because church leaders of a wide theological spectrum did not wish to refuse to be identified with evangelism and would not decline to take part, but they wanted those who came forward to be drawn into their churches. Some ministers to whom converts were as a result referred rebuffed them, telling them that it could not last. In fact it did last in a high proportion of people. Despite these problems, the isolation of evangelicals was never quite so strong again. Non-evangelicals began to see that evangelicals were needed as an evangelistic force in the churches, and that even an American 'fundamentalist' could not be totally dismissed.

Theological gains

In 1944, Lloyd-Jones had spoken at King's College, London, during a mission run by the CU. The Professor of New Testament Exegesis, R. V. G. Tasker, had attended.[19] By 1947, Tasker, who had been a moderate liberal, was willing to state that that meeting had revolutionized his whole life. He came out as a committed conservative, and offered his next book to the IVF.[20] He became a great help to theological students, publishing several theological monographs for them, including one on *The Biblical Doctrine of the Wrath of God*.[21] He was rudely cold-shouldered by his colleagues, and was even told to remember that one of his predecessors (F. D. Maurice) had been deprived of his post when he became out of step with the traditions of the faculty. Tasker agreed to edit the Tyndale New Testament Commentaries, writing the first one, on James, himself. It appeared in 1957. As King's was then one of the largest and most important theology departments, Tasker's editorship was significant. The Tyndale Commentaries were to develop into a significant resource. People had been told that to maintain a CE position they had to run away from the theological problems or become obscurantist. The fact that there were even a few able scholars who had clearly worked through the problems and come out strongly CE gave people confidence that even if one did not oneself have all the answers, it was not necessary to 'put one's intellect into pickle'. Tasker, when asked how he managed it, once replied: 'I have read the New Testament too much. The apostolic doctrine of the unique reliability and authority of the Bible is part of the whole warp and woof of the New Testament. You cannot reject it and keep the rest.'

Meanwhile, a group of younger men at Oxford, led by J. I. Packer and O. Raymond Johnston, were developing their theological skills and reading the Puritan writings, which were known by very few. Working with Martyn Lloyd-Jones, they started what became called the Puritan Studies Conference, an annual event in London, chaired by Lloyd-Jones and, until 1961, under the auspices of the Tyndale Fellowship. Its annual summer school met at Tyndale House and brought together many of the brightest of the younger CE theologians. Guided by DJ, it exposed them to some of the ablest American theologians from Westminster Theological Seminary. The Tyndale Fellowship developed a range of more specialized groups in Old Testament, New Testament, biblical archaeology and biblical theology, and after producing the *New Bible Commentary* in 1953, these set to work on the *New Bible Dictionary* (published in 1962). F. F. Bruce, J. I. Packer, R. V. G. Tasker and Donald Wiseman had the major input into the latter as the four consulting editors, as well as being substantial contributors. Wiseman was by now Professor of Assyriology in London, and had become a very important contributor to IVP literature as well as a much-valued speaker and a major influence in the policies of Tyndale House.

Both the *Commentary* and the *Dictionary* were major contributions to conservative literature in a way that it is hard for us now to appreciate. Apart from nineteenth-century or older commentaries, there were so few conservative ones available that many lay CEs did not own any, or use commentaries for leading Bible study groups and so on. In revised form, decades later, both volumes were to continue to be very widely distributed in Britain and America, and to be made available to theological students in the developing countries through the Evangelical Literature Trust (another of John Stott's initiatives). They still form the nucleus of the library of a very large number of ministers. In 1995 the *Dictionary* was to be translated into the Czech language, and to sell out in a few months.

Ecumenical issues

In his enthronement address as Archbishop of Canterbury in 1942, William Temple had given publicity to the term 'ecumenical'. He had said, 'Here is the great ground of hope for the coming days – this world-wide Christian fellowship, this ecumenical movement, as it is often called.'[22] He was not alone in thinking that it was a 'great ground of hope'. In the same year the British Council of Churches was created under his leadership, and, although plans were in hand for a World Council of Churches, the war did not allow its creation until 1948. It was a time of ecumenical optimism, but evangelicals were not enthusiastic. For a number of CEs ecumenism became the major issue, and they became strongly hostile because it inevitably downgraded doctrine in an effort to find a very wide unity in worship or experience. The official ecumenical organizations also seemed to present the threat of the creation of a super-church that would not give much place to doctrine and could be hostile to any strong truth-claims, allowing evangelicals to come in as only one rather curious specimen in a theological zoo.

There were signs in the literature that this fear was not unreasonable, though it was easy to exaggerate it. In 1953 the IVF published an address by Lloyd-Jones under the title *Maintaining the Evangelical Faith Today*. There was a slashing riposte in the *British Weekly* (then an important Christian paper). It was unsigned, giving it an appearance of being an editorial policy, though it seems to have been written by Nathaniel Micklem, the Principal of Mansfield College, Oxford. The article rightly recognized that the booklet was a call to keep to biblical orthodoxy and to repudiate the drift into eclectic ecumenism, represented by the BCC and WCC. Micklem wrote: 'The Inter-Varsity Fellowship, which, as utterly committed to the Gospel, might well be the spearhead of the Christian challenge to the world, is, in some places and where it follows the lead of Dr Lloyd-Jones, divisive, schismatic, obscurantist and quite unbiblical.' This gave warning that the WCC style of ecumenism was likely to be intolerant of anyone who made claim to revealed truth that might repudiate error as error. Lloyd-Jones replied in a letter in which he stated that, contrary to Micklem's suggestion that his position was due to his Calvinism, 'I have always asserted and argued as strongly as I could that evangelicals should not separate on the question of Calvinism and Arminianism. In the IVF . . . Arminians and Calvinists work most happily and harmoniously together, and it is my privilege to co-operate with all such.'[23]

Evangelicals, meanwhile, had their own ecumenism, bounded by the authority of Scripture. In fact, of course, the Evangelical Alliance had been created over a hundred years before, and there were numerous societies where evangelicals worked together harmoniously over a wide range of denominational loyalties. To them, denominational allegiances were now less important than they had been before the war, when very few Anglicans or Baptists would have changed over if they moved to a new town. A 'gospel ministry' was now seen as much more important than anything else, in the face of increasingly unorthodox teaching in many churches.

In 1952, the British Evangelical Council was formed to maintain a CE doctrinal witness as over against the official ecumenical bodies. Roland Lamb was its part-time Secretary from 1967, and the first full-time holder of that position from 1969. The BEC helped to support congregations that felt isolated or threatened by denominational leaders, whose rather starry-eyed ecumenical enthusiasm seemed to marginalize them and allow them no voice. It also gave a public witness for the essential maintenance of strong biblical doctrine. As it included the Free Church of Scotland, some small evangelical Presbyterian churches in Ireland and then from 1967 the Evangelical Movement of Wales and some independent churches, it could by 1981 claim to have 1,200 congregations in its membership, mostly of a fairly strongly Reformed character.

At the same time, the Fellowship of Independent Evangelical Churches, which had been started by E. J. Poole-Connor well before the war, grew in importance. Its aim was more pastoral than that of the BEC, and it linked up independent churches and mission halls in a fellowship of mutual help and advice. It was joined by a steady trickle of congregations which left their denominations. When, in 1967, Westminster Chapel left the Congregational Union and joined the FIEC (along with Above Bar Church in Southampton, where Leith Samuel was minister), it began to represent a growing and important section of evangelical church life. Lloyd-Jones had moved slowly in this, and was not the initiator. He regarded the BEC as the more significant body, though at first too negative; and was aware that while for him to leave his denomination would not cause any serious disadvantage, for small congregations to do so might cost much in the loss of buildings and manses as well as support from central funds. He did not wish to urge people to make sacrifices that he himself would not have to share.

The Evangelical Alliance was not so important at this stage, although the Billy Graham campaign had given it a much greater profile. Its wide scope left it without a very clear role in the minds of many evangelicals. It did not affiliate congregations (as well as individuals) until later.

Missionary concerns

In 1954, the SCM published (for the United Bible Societies) A. M. Chirgwin's *The Bible in World Evangelism*. This was the fruit of a three-year study to prepare a paper for the World Council of Churches Assembly at Evanston in 1954. It stressed 'the actual words of the Bible' in evangelism (p. 143). Stating that 'on more than one occasion a rediscovery of the Bible has been the accompaniment, if not the cause, of a new outburst of evangelistic activity and missionary advance', it asks: 'Is history going to repeat itself?' It summarizes its case with the comment: 'Biblical renewal and evangelistic advance appear to go together' (pp. 59, 63). The WCC did not seem to take the point.

The end of the war gave evangelicals great opportunities for work overseas in both government and missionary capacities. New high schools, technical colleges and universities were being created almost everywhere, and great changes in the younger nations that had been part of the British Empire offered numerous posts overseas in government employment. The IVF, which had a well-established Inter-Varsity Missionary Fellowship, started a work called the Inter-Varsity Overseas Fellowship, with its own conferences and newsletter, for those considering such openings. The idea of such service – now often called 'tentmaking' (Acts 18:3) – was relatively new except as what had been regarded as a very poor, second-class kind of service compared with 'proper missionary service'. The moving spirit here (with DJ) was Tony Wilmot,[24] at that time a civil servant in Ghana and later West African Co-ordinator of the Colonial Development Corporation based in Lagos. Wilmot in fact proved to be a remarkable evangelist and teacher for educated Africans, and became widely and affectionately known in Africa as 'Uncle Tony'. His emphasis, which is largely taken for granted today, was important, and represented a shift towards a more balanced idea of vocation.

Encouraged by Fred Crittenden, the IVF Graduates' Fellowship Secretary, many recent IVF graduates went out to teach in the new institutions and played a big part in establishing an evangelical student witness in them from the Far East to India, Africa and South America. Others taught in the high schools and, working with the Scripture Union, built up school CUs. Towards the end of this period nearly 10% of all graduates from CUs were going overseas. Overseas students also came to Britain in large numbers. Both these groups of students provided many future leaders of national churches. Several of the overseas students, such as Gottfried Osei-Mensah, became important in international activities[25] later.

In 1947 the International Fellowship of Evangelical Students was created,[26] largely built round the contacts that DJ had established, before and during the war, in co-operation with the Scandinavian movements equivalent to the IVF. DJ, who was an obvious first Secretary of the movement, managed to find someone else to do that: Stacey Woods from Canada. He found in Fred Crittenden an exceptionally gifted worker for overseas students in the UK, and sent Tony Wilmot on a tour of the African universities to explore the possibilities of work there. Lloyd-Jones became Chairman and, with Professor Carl Wisloff of Norway (who had in fact suggested the idea of such a fellowship in the first place before the war), the chief theologian of the IFES. The Scripture Union also developed its overseas work, especially in Africa. Here, from 1955, it was led by Nigel Sylvester, who had been converted in one of the Cambridge missions. Delegations from the growing movements in Europe and elsewhere came in considerable numbers to the IVF's large Swanwick conferences. They helped to give an international vision to British students, and were often inspiring as they wrestled with liberalism in much the same ways as the IVF had done ten years before.

1955

By 1955, evangelicals were clearly led by the conservatives, who had the initiatives in most areas. LEs were fading out. The SCM in the student world was contracting and tending to go towards a radical liberal stance. There were more CE churches, including a number in university towns that were attracting both Christian and non-Christian students. John Stott convened an annual conference for ministers in university towns (known as MUTS!), and encouraged suitable people to obtain such a ministry. CE congregations were growing in strength and in the doctrinal content of their ministry. CEs had lost any inferiority complex, were more confident of their message and much more evangelistically fruitful than they had been before the war, particularly among students and other thinking young people.

The high-church party in the Church of England was showing signs of weakness in that they were less confident of their authority. It was common for them to speak of the threefold authority of Scripture, tradition and reason. By now, however, they had accepted much of reason's undermining of the Bible and were in difficulties about the exact nature of the tradition, so that they were moving towards a more liberal position, depending on what could be rationally defended. A few were moving to a virtually Roman Catholic position (without accepting the authority of the pope).

Looking back on this period, it is clear that CEs were now much better able to keep their young people, many of whom remained strong in the faith. Their children often emerged a generation later as firm CEs, with a firmer and more confident grasp of the faith than had been the case before the war, and better able to evangelize their generation. There was no shrinking from theological debate or apologetic issues. In a way that had not been true before the war, the CEs felt able to confront the secular world and the theological establishment. David Bebbington expresses it as 'a broadening of the conservative Evangelical tradition. The postwar Evangelical renaissance was in fact a movement among those of firmly orthodox belief.'[27]

Classical evangelicalism was proving once more to be a very effective evangelizing force among all kinds of people, able to reach the educated as well as others with far more credibility than it had done for a long time. It was also training young Christians so that they were able to stand firm and to bring Christian influence into areas where evangelical voices had hardly been heard. That is not to suggest that there were none who withdrew from the CE community or lost faith altogether. There were some, but surveys done on CU members at this time showed that only about 5% of their members had not continued as active Christians ten years later. Those who stated that evangelical conversions would not last were largely mistaken.

5. CONSOLIDATION
1955–70

In the mid 1950s, the leadership of the evangelical cause was almost without exception in CE hands. Yet in spite of the apparent doctrinal unity and solidarity of the movement, significant divisions soon began to appear. Most of them arose, in different ways, out of evangelicals' more accepted position in the church scene and in the country. They were no longer having to fight quite so hard for a hearing, even if their doctrinal position was still constantly subject to attack and not infrequently to caricature. They had arrived as a recognized force in the church community. In the universities and in most of the colleges the CUs were now the main voice of Christian witness at the undergraduate level, to the dismay of theologically liberal observers.

This new strength brought with it the danger of self-congratulation and of ceasing to fight for the truth against error. Like the children of Israel in Judges 1, when they were strong (not when they were weak) it was easy to stop driving out the errors and to cease from contending for the faith. It was therefore a dangerous time for the evangelical cause. The history of God's people in the Old Testament shows repeatedly that it was when they were more comfortable that decline set in. Evangelical leadership at this time was, however, well aware of the danger and kept the priorities in place, even if some younger people did not.

Opposition
The theological establishment reacted to the increased strength of evangelicals in two contrasting ways. At the academic level they hit back vigorously. At a more pastoral level they tried to bring the evangelicals into partnership if they

would drop any insistence on truth and error within the church community.

When it was announced that Billy Graham had agreed to be the CICCU missioner in 1955, the opposition boiled over. A vigorous correspondence was started in *The Times* by Canon H. K. Luce of Durham. 'The recent increase of fundamentalism amongst university students cannot but cause concern to those whose work lies in religious education', he wrote. 'No branch of knowledge can make terms with an outlook which ignores the conclusions of modern scholarship in that particular department of knowledge . . . Universities exist for the advancement of learning; on what basis, therefore, can fundamentalism claim a hearing at Cambridge?' Various dignitaries entered the debate. John Stott, G. T. Manley, John Wenham and others replied. The correspondence was sufficiently important to be reprinted for publication as a booklet.[1] When the mission was over, but just before a CU mission in Durham University, A. M. Ramsey, who was at that time Bishop of Durham, wrote a blistering attack in his diocesan paper *The Bishoprick*, mentioning Billy Graham and the IVF.[2] He had just been nominated Archbishop of York and was before long to be Archbishop of Canterbury. Under the title of 'The Menace of Fundamentalism', he offered a caricature of an evangelistic meeting and continued: 'He [Billy Graham] has gone, our English fundamentalism remains. It is *heretical* . . . it is *sectarian*.' He more than hinted that he expected a 'backwash of moral casualties and disillusioned sceptics'. Ramsey was a relatively orthodox high-churchman (he had also been one of the most orthodox professors in the theology faculty at Cambridge), and the violence of his attack surprised people, but it exposed just how deeply the theologically minded establishment was opposed to evangelical doctrine.

In 1957, Gabriel Hebert, a respected high-church theological teacher, published a further attack in a book entitled *Fundamentalism and the Church of God*,[3] concentrating his polemic on the doctrine of Scripture and what he regarded as too low a view of the church and its sacraments. J. I. Packer replied in 1958 in what became an important resource for evangelicals for a long time: *'Fundamentalism' and the Word of God*.[4] This precipitated Packer into the position of a leading theologian and apologist for the evangelical cause.

The result of these debates was rather to strengthen than to weaken the convictions of the CEs. Most of them rather enjoyed the battle because they could see that they were contending for the faith once for all entrusted to the saints (Jude 3) against relative novelties in the Protestant community. As far as Anglican and Presbyterian CEs were concerned, they were contending for the position of the official formularies of their denominations – the Thirty-nine

Articles (which are moderately Calvinistic) and the Westminster Confession respectively. They were on strong ground. When one Anglican ordinand (Michael Griffiths) was questioned by the bishop and his examining chaplains about his theological position, because doubts had been raised, he was able at the end of the discussion to say that it seemed that he was the only one in the room who believed in the Articles (to which, of course, they had all had to give assent at their ordination).[5]

Ecumenical approaches

J. I. Packer, who had started at Oxford playing the clarinet in a jazz band, had been converted through the OICCU (Oxford Inter-Collegiate Christian Union) in his first year (1946). When he became an OICCU librarian, he discovered the Puritan writers among their books and soon became a leader in a small group of more Reformed students in the OICCU. He became a powerful advocate for a more doctrinal evangelicalism, not so much by direct argument for it as by showing that doctrine was necessary for apologetics and for daily life. He did not stress his Calvinism. Like a number of others who discovered the riches of Reformation and Puritan writings, he was speaking from the standpoint of a *biblical* doctrine of God as sovereign in revelation and redemption. Neither he nor others of his position liked to adopt a label of a party kind other than being biblical Christians. Packer was also an Anglican, and so bridged one of the widening gaps between CEs in the different churches.

At the same time, a number of ecumenical leaders were making a totally different approach. They stressed that the CE position was basically acceptable as one point of view and urged that the CEs should come into the great worldwide network to make their particular contribution, and not try to work in a relatively small and uninfluential minority. In particular, they should bring their evangelistic abilities and vision to work with all other Christians for the evangelization of Britain. Following the broad platform of the Billy Graham crusades in London and Scotland, they were optimistic, though Graham had in fact preserved the preaching in the hands of CEs. Some CEs were flattered by this approach, and relieved, for the first time in a generation or more, to be treated with such respect. Others, remembering the history of groups that had slipped into theological vagueness when their leaders had accepted the position of an evangelical wing of a broad-spectrum witness, were much more cautious.

On the Free Church side, the position of Lloyd-Jones and some others on co-operation hardened, not only out of considered principle, but out of experience. In 1956, the British Council of Churches made a start with discussions between their representatives and some CE leaders including Lloyd-Jones, John Stott and Leith Samuel. They proposed that the only real difference between them was over the doctrine of the Bible. As the discussions covered other doctrines, it became clear, as Lloyd-Jones had in fact predicted, that they were in disagreement over almost every aspect of doctrine – the atonement, the new birth (was it at baptism?), the doctrine of humanity, the fall, who is a Christian, the church, the sacraments, the person and authority of Christ, and much more. Stott withdrew early on. Lloyd-Jones attended patiently, until finally in 1961 the BCC stopped the talks, partly because they were not producing the desired unity and partly because very few of their representatives now attended. The exchanges had served only to underline the fact that the disagreements were fundamental to the nature of the gospel that was to be preached.[6]

In Scotland, the relatively small Baptist Union left the ecumenical bodies and has not rejoined to this day, though while their position was unsettled their largest congregation (Charlotte Chapel in Edinburgh) left them and has remained independent.

Evangelical divisions

Probably there will always be differences of view about the degree of involvement in mixed denominations that is possible without compromise. It depends partly on temperament, but even more on upbringing. What to some people is a path of opportunity for evangelical influence in a loved denomination (often one in which they were converted) is to others a compromising of truth. The resulting differences of policy tend to lead to division and lack of appreciation of those who move in the other direction. There are also problems and dangers peculiar to both separation and involvement.

That some CE Anglicans were moving in a direction different from that of the rest of their CE brothers and sisters emerged sharply in 1965, when Packer edited a book, to which he contributed, under the title *All in Each Place: Towards Reunion in England*.[7] The ten contributors mainly stressed the concept of a national church. To Free Church readers it represented a desire to justify working more closely with non-evangelicals, and particularly with the more orthodox high-church leaders in the Church of England. It spoke of all members of the Church of England as if they were to be regarded as true

Christians. This was an acute disappointment to many Free Church CEs, particularly as Packer had been working so closely with Lloyd-Jones and other Free Church people in the Puritan Conference and other activities.

Then, in October 1966, Lloyd-Jones spoke at a preliminary meeting for the National Evangelical Assembly convened by the Evangelical Alliance.[8] John Stott was in the chair. Lloyd-Jones made a plea to all evangelicals to put their fellowship with other evangelicals above other church loyalties. He used the phrase 'come out', and spoke movingly of the need for sacrifice if necessary. He had to say repeatedly afterwards that he had neither then nor at any time advocated a new denomination. John Stott, fearing that some of those present would immediately go home and write letters of resignation from their denominations, rose to say that he could not agree with what had been proposed. The 'remnant', to which Lloyd-Jones had referred, was within the Old Testament 'church' and not outside it. The weakness of Lloyd-Jones's position was that he was not proposing any particular practical solution to the problems. He had not suggested any plan of action. He was stating the principle. There was no widely acceptable body to unite CEs. The Evangelical Alliance affiliated only individuals until 1965, and the BEC and FIEC could not accept churches in mixed denominations and in any case held no attraction for Anglicans. Lloyd-Jones was taken to be making a plea that was no longer acceptable to those Anglicans (and some in other churches) who believed that now was a time for further involvement in their denominations, and not the reverse. It was a painful event and left a painful memory for many. It has often been discussed, with various interpretations. What it represented, however, soon became clearer.

In *England*, the first National Evangelical Anglican Congress took place in 1967 at Keele. The idea originated with a group of scattered clergy in the north of England, led by Raymond Turvey. John Stott had a key role in planning it, in chairing sessions and in drawing up the resolutions. A thousand representatives of churches attended. The whole occasion was firmly in the hands of CEs, and represented a reaffirmation of CE positions. What was most noticed at the time, and in subsequent debates, was the evident commitment of most if not all of those present not only to remain in the Church of England but to play a more active part in the denomination at all levels. Keele has often been seen as a more or less irreversible commitment to be loyal to the denomination and to make it a priority to try to influence it from within. Most of those concerned valued the Church of England as 'the national church'. To those outside the Church of England, it seemed to be an agreement to value fellowship with people of all sorts of heretical views, who happened to be Anglicans, more highly than fellowship and co-operation with other CEs. The short paragraph in the Keele Statement about relationships with evangelicals in other churches did not seem to require any action.[9] The situation led to a temporary breakdown of fellowship and even of friendship across that denominational boundary. Only a few Anglicans seemed to care much about that. The majority had the bit between their teeth and were excited by the prospect of exercising a growing evangelical influence in the Church of England. They hoped to bring it back to a biblical faith, as represented at least by the Thirty-nine Articles. Evangelicalism, they held, was the true faith of the Church of England.

In 1960, however, some who did care greatly about doctrine and its out-working created Latimer House in Oxford as a centre for Anglican evangelical theological study and writing. John Stott was Chairman, and J. I. Packer and John Wenham were both to be on the staff soon after. It has continued to be staunchly CE, but has never been a major influence on Anglican thinking, in spite of some good publications. The Thirty-nine Articles were gradually dropping into the background and evangelicals soon ceased to appeal to them.

In retrospect, one can see that the strong presence of the high-church tradition in the Church of England, which some evangelicals were beginning to regard as no longer an enemy but an ally in fighting the liberal tendencies, was pushing evangelicals to go the same way if they wished to be accepted and listened to. That was not altogether a conscious process, but it was said then, as it is now, that if they were to exercise any influence in the Church of England they had to accept some more traditionally high-church emphases. In liturgical revision (which had produced the first alternative services in 1965), for instance, they were later to accept a communion service that they agreed was not their ideal, because it was the best they could get. It was, however, much sounder in important respects than it would have been if they had not been involved in framing it. (The Anglican Church in Wales seems to have ended up with a communion service that is easier to make strongly evangelical.) Wherever the highlight of the service becomes 'the Peace', where people greet one another, there is the danger of a shift from the emphasis of the 1662 service – with its stress not on our unity but on the totally undeserved grace and mercy of God in the death of Christ.

In 1960 a small private IVF Anglican policy group, which included Alan Stibbs and of which I was Secretary, went public (and independent of the IVF) as the Church of England Evangelical Council, with John Stott as Chairman and Dick Lucas as Secretary. At that stage it was clearly CE, but later, as it drew in a wider range of evangelicals, it began to lose that clarity. When Alan Stibbs and I were invited to attend a meeting in 1971, he left almost in tears at what he felt was its departure from his hopes for it.

John Stott's influence had by this period become of huge importance, especially in the Church of England. He had written numerous books and articles with a large circulation. He had travelled extensively in the UK, and increasingly abroad also, for university missions and for lectures, especially on preaching.[10] At Keele, aged forty-six, he became the acknowledged leader of the evangelical Anglican cause, and he was soon to hold that same position worldwide. He was a constant advocate of expository preaching. Some highly respected preachers would take a text and rephrase it in a sentence, preaching on their sentence rather than on the text. Stott insisted on preaching on the text or passage itself, and on proclaiming what it actually said and implied within an overall biblical framework. While he was not afraid of necessary controversy – as indicated by his 1970 book *Christ the Controversialist*[11] – he won people most by the positive statement of the truth. He was not abrasive, as so many evangelical controversialists had been.

The Keele Statement had another surprise for many. It stated that 'We determine to work towards the practice of a weekly celebration of the sacrament as the central corporate service of the church'. Where this has been adopted, it has effectively closed off the morning service (usually) as an evangelistic opportunity, because it was clearly inappropriate to invite known non-Christians to participate. Services began to approximate to the Brethren pattern of one, usually liturgical, Sunday service for Christians, with the other service being much freer and having little respect for the Prayer Book liturgy. Not many parishes actually did what was recommended, and those that did had some difficulty in reversing it if they had good opportunities of reaching the unchurched and a heart for evangelism through both their Sunday services.

What was forgotten by many non-Anglicans, however, was that under the leadership of John Stott, Keele was a very powerful affirmation of the CE doctrinal position as *the* evangelical position. Many had too-short memories of the position before the war to realize how revolutionary this was.

In *Scotland* and *Ireland* in the Presbyterian churches, the same problems did not arise. There were growing CE groupings in both countries. In Scotland, they mainly but not exclusively revolved round those who had been influenced by William Still and his circle, including James Philip and George Philip. Of these a good number had been converted or helped theologically through the IVF.

They, however, had never been in doubt about their denominational loyalties or their hope of restoring their churches to evangelical positions, and the doctrinal divergencies were never so extreme as in the Church of England. The Westminster Confession seems to have had a stronger influence among the Presbyterians than the Thirty-nine Articles with Anglicans, and to have prevented the more blatantly unevangelical extremes from having much impact.

The Church of Ireland was unique in Anglicanism in being uniformly low church, and the title 'evangelical' was loosely used. The Irish Prayer Book, which was in several ways sounder than the English one, was in universal use. Eucharistic vestments and coloured stoles were never used, and this gave an impression to visitors of an evangelical church. When, however, Herbert Carson wrote in the *Church of England Newspaper* that 'it is possible to be "low church" without being evangelical',[12] he created a storm, because people did not want to make that distinction too clearly. Northern Ireland remained much more 'religious' than the rest of the United Kingdom.[13] Apologetics did not seem so urgent, and much evangelism continued in the tradition of Willy Nicholson and Moody (and Billy Graham), quite effectively in that context.

In *Wales* the pressure on Presbyterian CE congregations was more fierce, and some left the denomination, including its largest congregation at Heath in Cardiff. From 1967 the Evangelical Movement of Wales was able to affiliate churches in mixed denominations, but very few took advantage of this. There was a small fellowship of evangelical ministers in the Anglican Church in Wales, which was carefully encouraged by John Stott during his repeated visits to his remote cottage in Pembrokeshire (where he wrote his many books), though the cottage soon became too small for these meetings. The historical tensions between Anglican and Free churches in Wales, however, had allowed hardly any fellowship across that boundary since the disestablishment of the Church in Wales, so that the EMW's fellowship was a gain. That there were real evangelicals in the Church in Wales was a source of almost incredulity to many non-Anglicans in the Principality.

One major loss in these changes was that the stronger emphasis on doctrine that had been such a feature of the previous twenty years was weakened in the Church of England when Lloyd-Jones and other Free Church leaders, who had contributed much to it, were no longer listened to by Anglicans. The Westminster Fellowship was closed, and restarted after a while with terms of membership that effectively excluded those in doctrinally mixed denominations.

These divisions did not hinder co-operation in the interdenominational bodies such as SU, the IVF, the EA, Keswick and the OMF, but it planted a suspicion among many Free Church people that Anglican evangelicals would be soft on doctrine and more interested in being involved in the Church of England than in a clear doctrinal stand.[14]

Literature developments

The IVF's publications department, which adopted the name Inter-Varsity Press in 1968, was by now the most important CE publisher. Donald Wiseman was writing with authority on biblical archaeology and related Old Testament subjects. Like many others he owed much to the encouragement and friendship of DJ and the stimulus of W. J. Martin, who never seemed able to produce substantial written material himself, but helped many to work on scholarly tasks. Donald Guthrie, who was by then the Vice-Principal of London Bible College, was stirred into writing by Ronald Inchley, and Guthrie's *Introduction to the New Testament* became an indispensable resource for students.[15]

In 1968, Francis Schaeffer's first two books were published. His visits to the UK before that had created an appetite for whatever he wrote, especially an overflowing IVF Graduates' Fellowship conference in 1965, where his talks became the basis of his book *Escape from Reason*.[16] His subsequent visits reinforced his influence. He was a strong Calvinistic thinker and staunchly conservative in theology. His influence was and still is considerable, especially in apologetics. He steadied the CE community, giving a fresh vision for orthodoxy when some were tempted to wander from it. Schaeffer was also strong on the need not only to think biblically but also to live biblically, and to relate in a truly Christian way to others. He seemed, however, too philosophical to have a wide appeal, and he was not particularly skilled as a speaker at public meetings. He was superb in talking to individuals and in discussion in a group. Many people are still indebted to his analysis of the drift of modern thought and how to respond to it. The L'Abri centres and its speakers continue to spread his influence in the 1990s. Those who heard his lectures will not forget his graphic descriptions of the danger of separating an 'upper-storey' spirituality from a 'lower-storey' material and practical world. He helped many also to a more biblical assessment of humanity. One of his repeated statements was 'Man is not junk'. He did a great deal to encourage a bold entry into the areas covered by the media, and, together with his friend Hans Rookmaaker, created a more positive attitude to the arts. His approach was also important in evangelical apologetics, and among other things he saw the dangers of separating spiritual experience from truth. He emphasized 'true truth', and warned of the dangers of a merely 'upper-storey' experience that did not arise from biblical revelation, as was becoming common under the cultural pressure of the times. He helped to remove the lingering fear in CE circles of intellectual and theological involvement (though this has returned to some extent in the 1990s, especially in some charismatic circles).

The Reformed Christian philosophy of Dooyeweerd and Vollenhofen was introduced at this time from Holland, but it was not able to arouse more than a passing interest in most people because of its difficulty, and because of the lack of interest in philosophy both in Christian circles and in the country as a whole. It also seemed to some, myself included, to put philosophy above theology and thereby to avoid the necessity of going to the Bible first of all – and last of all. Van Til's writings, from Westminster Theological Seminary in the USA, probably had more influence at this stage in Reformed circles, especially in Ireland.

The Banner of Truth Trust, led by Iain Murray, published its first two books in 1958 and soon had a considerable following. The books were heavily subsidized at that stage. Because they and *The Banner of Truth* magazine (started in 1955) were seen as representing an extreme Calvinist position, they were not read much by Anglicans or Methodists, but circulated widely in Wales, Ireland and Scotland. The Trust made some of the best of the older Reformed classics available again as examples of a pastorally warm theology. The Puritan and other Reformed literature that was being published was heady stuff for many who had had a relatively thin doctrinal diet, especially the more thoughtful younger readers.

Confusion began to arise over the need for and the nature of evangelism. Hyper-Calvinism appeared, and Lloyd-Jones found himself warning of the dangers of a purely intellectual Christianity. When one student stated that he got more out of his 'quiet time' by reading Calvin's *Institutes* than by reading the Bible, something had clearly gone wrong. Packer's *Evangelism and the Sovereignty of God*[17] was a wise and effective corrective for many.

Doctrinal emphases

The whole evangelical community in England was tending to drift apart into a Reformed, predominantly non-Anglican wing and a less doctrinally minded majority. The former had to avoid the danger of becoming arid. Whenever people spoke of 'preaching the doctrines of grace', there was fear that they were just preaching doctrines. But the latter grouping was in danger of a loss of doctrinal thinking because they cut themselves off from some of the sources of stimulus in that direction. Evangelicals in all sections expounded Scripture with faithfulness and warmth, but at very different levels of doctrinal content, depending on their reading and the circles in which they moved. Theological education rarely left people time to read the great theologians and expositors of the past. For those who had the appetite and made time for it, that had to wait until later, when in the ministry.

In retrospect, there is no doubt that much of the renewed emphasis on biblical doctrine had come from those of a more definitely Reformed theology, such as Lloyd-Jones, Packer and Schaeffer. In any case, traditional evangelical Anglicanism, as represented by John Stott (who for many years read the Thirty-nine Articles in church on every anniversary of his ordination), is properly described as moderate Calvinism in many of its features. It is not popular today to admit any indebtedness to Calvinism (or to Lutheran theology), because Calvinism particularly has been represented in terms of some of its extremes. In any case, it is not so much to those Reformers that these people looked as to the undoubtedly biblical truths that they recovered and which had to some extent been lost sight of again. These aspects of biblical teaching were now fed back into evangelical thinking, and did much to equip people for the greater responsibilities and opportunities that they faced in the professions and in the churches. Where they were subsequently lost there would be a real danger of slipping again into a pietism that lacked the theological tools to grapple with wider intellectual issues.

The evangelical world has to acknowledge that some of the emphases that we now value, and even take for granted, came from the recovery of Reformation thinking at this stage. The much stronger emphasis on the character of God and his providential rule; the emphasis on the relative but positive value of the created order; the vision of vocation as including every useful occupation, and the use of the concept of 'common grace' (though not always under that name because of its ambiguity) were only some of the now accepted mainstream elements of CE thinking. These had also provided the theological basis for a new emphasis on social ethics and for a fresh approach to many questions in the professions. Schaeffer, for instance, was the first evangelical to publish a book in the UK on the environment, even if it was not his best.[18] The influence of premillennialism had also begun to be replaced by an amillennial view that put efforts to improve society in a positive light and relegated to the sidelines the speculative and sometimes heated debates about the second coming of Christ, freeing evangelical scholarship for more constructive matters.

Lloyd-Jones had a major influence in helping the Christian Medical Fellowship to establish a good, principled approach. In the scientific field the influence of Professor R. Hooykaas, from the Free University of Amsterdam (a Calvinistic foundation), working with Donald MacKay (with his background in the Free Church of Scotland), moulded the thinking of Christians in science and rescued them from a more simplistic and pietistic approach. Books and monographs by these two had appeared from 1957, and MacKay's *Christianity in a Mechanistic Universe* (1965) and *The Clockwork Image* (1974)[19] established a fresh and positive, rather than defensive, theological stance in relation to science. The Schoolteachers' Section of the Graduates' Fellowship grew in numbers, and in 1971 amalgamated with the older, more pietistic Teachers' Prayer Fellowship, and the Scripture Union's mailing list of teachers who were helping school CUs, to form the Association of Christian Teachers.

In the field of the media, where the IVF had struggled to help art students, the frequent visits of Professor Hans Rookmaaker (from the same Dutch Calvinistic university) to the art students' conferences and small groups in the colleges provided a breakthrough not only for students but also for the thinking of all evangelicals about the arts. He ran L'Abri Fellowship in Holland and was a close friend of Francis Schaeffer's. His 1970 *Modern Art and the Death of a Culture*[20] began to fill what was an almost total void in evangelical literature. This is not to suggest that the books were always the main influences. Publications, however, reached a much wider public than the work of numerous study groups and think-tanks that were in action in various areas.

There had for a while been a lively discussion group in which David Winter, who was then editor of the journal *Crusade*, was a co-ordinating factor. Independently, the IVF had appointed its first staffworker for the art and music colleges in 1965, and in 1968 held the first of a series of conferences for art students with Professor Rookmaaker as the main speaker. He showed great skill in looking at the students' work and encouraging them even when he was not very impressed. The actor Nigel Goodwin was converted in 1962 through a tent mission on Wimbledon Common run under the banner of the Children's Special Service Mission (SU).[21] Also in 1965 the popular singer Cliff Richard was converted, largely through a Crusader group whose leaders he knew and who included David Winter. Both these high-profile people were urged by some Christians to give up their work and enter the ministry or teaching, but were helped to a positive view of using the gifts that they had as a Christian vocation. The influence of Schaeffer's thinking in L'Abri and contact with Rookmaaker helped greatly here. Almost certainly the evangelical world of the 1930s would have been negative about this decision, and a number still had doubts. There were now, however, an openness and an attempt to think biblically about everything that could be seen as a God-given gift. In 1968, the IVF's conference for technical and art-college students was on 'Vocation', with Rookmaaker as one of the speakers. Several of those influenced by it took a lead in the art field. The most practical outcome of these discussions was the Arts Centre Group and their home in London established in 1970.[22]

There was a ferment of activity and fresh thought now that evangelicals had the doctrinal and intellectual tools and the confidence to grapple with such things. It is significant that in most of the fields where there was development, the focus was not on one or two individuals but on a group of people who had come to be concerned more or less independently, and then had found one another through their churches, Crusader classes, the IVF, L'Abri, or some other grouping.

Evangelism

It was a fruitful time in evangelism. Michael Green's evangelistic books had a big circulation, starting with *Man Alive!* and then *Runaway World* and *Jesus Spells Freedom*.[23] Television had not yet reduced the reading habits of young people much, and non-Christians would read these paperbacks and other literature, giving them at least some basic understanding of the truths needed as a background for gospel preaching. Friendship evangelism by very young Christians was greatly helped when they were able to give a book.

Smaller leaflets were produced for the technical colleges and had a very big circulation. This was not a promising field, since most students lived at home and, if they were Christians, continued to be heavily involved in their local church. Nevertheless, CUs multiplied and saw a very encouraging number converted. In the technical, art and agricultural colleges that came under the Technical Colleges Christian Fellowship, there were only thirty-five CUs in 1956 when Arthur Pont became the Secretary. Many were started rather timorously and ran only with the help of a lecturer. When Pont left to become the Home Director of the Bible and Medical Missionary Fellowship (now Interserve) in 1967, there were 350 CUs, and hundreds had been converted, producing some fine missionaries and other Christian workers at home and abroad.

Social concern

Keele had another effect that was less noticed at the time. Among the papers that were required reading for the congress was one by Norman Anderson under the title *Christian Worldliness: The Need and Limits of Christian Involvement*.[24] Like other papers, it was the result of some previous discussions and represented a change of emphasis for CEs. The statement issued at the end of the congress affirmed confidently that 'Evangelism and compassionate service belong together in the mission of God'. This would have been extremely doubtful before the war. Anderson published a fuller treatment the following year in *Into the World*,[25] and A. N. Triton's[26] *Whose World?* appeared from IVP in 1970. John Stott's very considerable influence came in a chapter in his 1970 book *Christ the Controversialist*. Before that, however, the IVF had published Fred Catherwood's *The Christian in Industrial Society* in 1964. That book was the result of a study group set up by the IVF's Graduates' Fellowship, which had met over several years under Catherwood's chairmanship. He followed it in 1969 with his *The Christian Citizen*.[27] These were only some of several attempts to get evangelicals to give more attention to the application of their faith not only to personal ethics but to social ethics as well. Catherwood put down a useful marker that distinguished the approach from liberal thinking that had made it suspect: 'There is, therefore, no "social *gospel*". The gospel is addressed to the individual. Society collectively cannot be redeemed. It can, however, be reformed according to the law of God. There is a "social *law*".'[28]

The negative attitude to social thinking and involvement was changing. It carried with it a much more positive attitude to 'secular' vocations as equally valuable in God's sight as what had been called 'full-time Christian work'. If *all* work was to be full-time for God, that idea would not do. People had to change their vocabulary and talk about 'full-time Christian ministry'. The superior position of the latter began to be eroded, though many ministers still measured their effectiveness by the number from their congregation who entered the ministry or went abroad as missionaries, and gave little help to those who wanted to know how to be better at their ordinary jobs as Christians. (At that time most theological students came straight from school or university, and ministers thus had no experience of secular employment.) For that kind of help, people had to look to the professional groups such as the Christian Medical Fellowship and Association of Christian Teachers. The Workers' Christian Fellowship, aiming more at the shop floor, never went far towards Christian thinking about the problems.

The change in outlook is illustrated by a correspondent who said that she had always thought of teaching simply as a means of evangelism, and that this literature had given her a new vision for being a good teacher. Another wrote that he felt that if he was a really committed Christian, he would have to be a minister or a missionary, but as it was he was 'only a banker'. It took him a while before he could say that he now had a new enthusiasm for his job.

All this was pure gain, but it posed the question of the relationship of social concern to evangelism, which continued to be debated in the next periods. Keele certainly put these questions firmly on the agenda for discussion and action in the Church of England, though the change preceded Keele and was wider than the Church of England. While Keswick and the more pietistic end of the evangelical spectrum largely ignored these issues, the more doctrinally minded bodies such as the British Evangelical Council began to introduce such topics at its conferences. The Presbyterians, especially in Scotland with their more Reformed tradition, did not have the same problems about the place of social action as did many others.

Since 1959, the Evangelical Alliance had been receiving gifts for relief work. Keele gave further emphasis to such concerns, and in 1968 the Evangelical Alliance set up TEAR Fund (The Evangelical Alliance Relief Fund),[29] which quickly grew into a major agency of philanthropic activity under the dynamic leadership of George Hoffman (between 1968 and 1989). It worked, in large measure, through the existing evangelical churches and missionary societies. It did not engage in political activity; to preserve its charitable status it could not do so. It therefore did not contribute greatly to the debates about Christian political involvement. It did, however, bring before the evangelical community such vivid pictures of poverty and deprivation that it naturally raised questions in people's minds about the structures of society that cause such conditions.[30] This positive initiative and its massive support would have been almost impossible in the 1930s. It represented a more biblically balanced position about social involvement than had been possible before the war.

These developments all represented a working out of a CE position into areas where for a long time there had been little evangelical thinking. There was now a great need for evangelical initiatives, and far less in the way of impressive alternative Christian views than there had been. Such thinking and literature helped considerably in keeping the rising generation active in evangelical circles, and in reducing the temptation to move out and disown their more pietistic background.

Charismatic influences

During this period the influence of charismatic experience, which hitherto had been largely confined to the Pentecostal denominations, spread into the other church groupings. Michael Harper came into this experience in 1963, while he was still a curate to John Stott at All Souls, Langham Place. He left in 1964 and set up the Fountain Trust to spread such an emphasis especially in the Church of England. The Fountain Trust did not invite Pentecostal ministers on to its platform, and the two streams never worked together. The Methodist and Baptist Revival Fellowships were influenced by charismatic renewal in the late 1960s, and this weakened their appeal to some CEs in those denominations. Fairly strong divisions were created over the issue almost wherever it appeared in these early years of its influence. John Stott's IVF booklet *The Baptism and Fullness of the Holy Spirit* (1964) aligned him firmly against some of the language and emphases being used. Lloyd-Jones' position was more ambiguous, because he was anxious not to discourage any openness to a fresh work of the Holy Spirit in the individual's life, quoting certain experiences of some of the Puritans. But he never identified himself at all with the renewal movement. By 1970 there was no certainty as to how things would develop. The story really belongs to the next periods. Charismatics were hardly in evidence at Keele. By 1977, at the second National Evangelical Anglican Congress, held in Nottingham, they were a visible section of those present. Outside the mainstream denominations, charismatic house churches (now called 'new churches') began to multiply in several networks, each led by a small group or individual. The Pentecostal denominations also grew in strength and in the number of congregations.

Cultural changes

The 1960s have often been cited as the period of greatest social and cultural change in this century. The decade has been called 'the hopefully structureless sixties'.[31] The young people were the children of wartime or the years soon after the war, when discipline was difficult and much more lax than it had been before. Rebellion was in the air. The period has been described in these terms: 'Young people of the 1960s, in Britain as in America, were turning in large numbers to a counter-culture, the world of hippies and drop-outs, drugs and flower power. "Make love not war" was the slogan of the day.'[32] Theodore Roszak's book *The Making of a Counter-Culture*[33] summarized much of it. Morality began to slide dramatically, and divorce to increase. A certain arrogance of youth appeared, and questioned more drastically than before all that their elders said.

On the whole, evangelicals dealt with this well, though it was not long before divorce and premarital sex began to appear among churchgoers, including some in evangelical churches. What one 'felt' was regarded as more important than what one believed, and the great aim was to find 'fulfilment' in one's job, one's marriage and one's social life. It has been called the 'me generation'. These tendencies have never been reversed to date. One result was that youth groups in many churches became inward-looking 'fellowships' and lost their previous emphasis on teaching and evangelism. It was hoped that worship would be a powerful evangelistic witness in itself, though it was seen largely in terms of a lot of singing, and outsiders rarely knew what to make of the jargon. David Wells, writing about the North American scene, says: 'Thus was biblical truth eclipsed by the self and holiness by wholeness.'[34] It took determination to correct the cultural drift. These and other changes affected other sections of the churches more than the evangelicals. The Kingsway Hall, where Donald Soper had preached for so long, was sold, and one of the two very high-church theological colleges, Kelham, was closed in 1970. Professor Adrian Hastings (a Roman Catholic historian) wrote of evangelicals that 'as a group they came through the sixties in far the best shape'[35] compared with other sections of the churches.

Radical theology

Into this situation J. A. T. Robinson, a liberal bishop, injected his book *Honest to God*[36] in 1963. It had enormous sales, though most readers had to admit, if asked, that they had not finished it. Its debunking of many traditional ways of speaking, such as the credal statement 'He [Jesus Christ] came down from heaven', appealed to the current iconoclasm and made it seem acceptable to be radical in theology. Robinson was, after all, a bishop! He fitted in with the cultural outlook in speaking of God, not as the One to reckon with and the eternal Creator, but as 'the ground of our being'. He was left with hardly anything of substance as a focus for faith, or any framework of doctrine. As one non-Christian who read the book remarked, he seemed to be someone who had reasoned himself out of faith. As might be expected, he followed radical theology with radical ethics in his *Christian Morals Today*.[37] Joseph Fletcher's *Situation Ethics*,[38] pointing in the same direction to a radically liberal stance in ethics, appeared in 1966. Both (for instance) justified premarital sex where there was real love, and did so in the name of Christianity. It became harder to maintain a clear biblical line against this combination of cultural trend and popular theology. Evangelicals, however, fought back quite effectively. J. I.

Packer published on both the theology and the ethics, and others joined in. There was no weakening of the stand for biblical truth and life among evangelicals. Hastings comments: 'Liberal theology captured the theologians but never really reached the pews . . . In the seventies, as a consequence, the gap between theologians and the pews was greater than ever.'[39]

By 1970, the growth of the evangelical community had resulted in the development of considerable variety within a fairly firmly CE framework. This led some to regret the cohesion that had been a strong feature of the movement in days when every step of the way was strongly contested and all were together in an exhilarating battle for the truth. Enjoying the luxury of their own special interests and concerns, there was less unity, and differences of doctrinal emphasis were beginning to emerge, some of them appearing to lead away from the CE priorities. Success was leading to the danger of some self-congratulation – not among the leaders, such as John Stott, but in the rank and file.

6. MORE ADVENTURE, LESS UNITY 1970–80

If the 1970s seem not to have given rise to any totally new trends, they did witness the accentuation of those trends that had emerged since the war. By 1970, evangelicals were much stronger numerically and were still led by conservatives, but they were less united than they had been on church policies and on some theological issues. They were fully committed to the final authority and reliability of the Bible, and were actively exploring the application of biblical truth to every area of life, from economics and politics to abortion. Some of them were rising to positions of considerable responsibility in the churches and in public life. They were mostly convinced that social action was a Christian duty that went along with evangelism, though the exact relationship between the two was still being debated. Their strength led a number of commentators to talk of them as 'having the ball at their feet', exactly as they had done in 1850. The clearly CE Principal of Oak Hill College, Maurice Wood, was made a bishop in 1971.[1] In 1975 both Archbishops (Donald Coggan and Stuart Blanch) were evangelicals, though neither would have called himself CE. Others gained positions of influence in public affairs. Norman Anderson, for instance, became vice-chairman of Lord Longford's study group on pornography, as well as chairman of the House of Laity of the Church of England Synod.[2] Interestingly, Anderson was also a former missionary. As president of the CICCU (1930–31), he had refused an academic career in law to go as a missionary to Egypt. His excellent Arabic drew him into important war service with legal implications, and after the war he returned to be Warden at Tyndale House, was drawn into teaching Islamic law, and ended up in one of the top academic legal jobs in the UK – Director

97

of the Institute of Advanced Legal Studies in London. Others had a voice in places where they could have some influence in church or state, and were able to carry such responsibilities much more effectively than their predecessors would have done.

The local church scene

The cultural changes and the loss of biblical background in the population meant that evangelism was becoming more difficult again, though much good work was being done. The gap between the Christian and non-Christian outlooks and lifestyles had widened. The Bible was being taught less in schools. Preachers could no longer assume that their hearers had an awareness of sin, and, if they had, they were often not sure that it mattered very much. It was not easy to persuade people to come to church, and its services seemed, to many of the younger generation at least, to belong to a different world from the one they lived in. Billy Graham's approach and the quick move to an appeal was less appropriate, though many still held it as an ideal.

Added to this, the younger church members knew far less. Family prayers became rare and the habit of a 'quiet time' had declined substantially. A short while before, a widely circulated book on the subject had contained the slogan 'No Bible, no breakfast'. Now, however, most young people skipped breakfast! That sort of disciplined life was not popular, and they got out of bed just in time for the first lesson, lecture or appointment. 'Self-control' had become the least popular part of the whole fruit of the Spirit. Many converted people were almost biblically illiterate. This left them very vulnerable when they moved away from a warm fellowship or were subjected to erroneous teaching.

The habit of learning verses or passages by heart also became uncommon, even in Sunday schools. This was accelerated by the multiplicity of Bible versions that were coming into use, so that the precise words of the text were not uniform as they had been when the Authorized Version reigned supreme. The AV was still being used by the more conservative churches, though its language was hard for some to understand, and the absence even of paragraphs in most editions meant that the epistles read like a string of disconnected verses. J. B. Phillips' translation of the epistles had appeared in 1947, and his New Testament in 1958, but it was rarely used in public worship. In 1952 the complete Revised Standard Version was published, but, due to strong criticism of a few important theologically slanted passages, did not find wide acceptance in CE congregations. Nevertheless, because it was the best recent scholarly version, it was the usual study text in theological colleges and faculties. Few CEs used the New English Bible, completed in 1970. The full Good News Bible appeared in 1976, deliberately using a very limited vocabulary. Ministers began to make their own translations as they went along, or to use several versions as seemed best for the particular passage.

It was only when the New International Version appeared (NT 1973, complete Bible 1978) that many CE churches switched to a version that has become standard in a wide circle. Using and learning the exact words of the Bible has never recovered its former place, even in Sunday schools, and this is a serious loss. Many ordinary church members have never read considerable parts of the Bible, and cannot find important books without looking in the contents page, let alone find a verse to quote in a discussion with a non-Christian.

This has created a greater gap between ministers and those in the pew, because a knowledge of the words in which the basic truths in Scripture are expressed was too often assumed. Biblical phraseology, such as 'the blood of the Lamb', and songs about 'Zion', for instance, could baffle the newcomer to church in a way that it had not done previously. The problems of communicating the message increased.

Television had become a major factor in life, with its emphasis on entertainment and the intrusion into Christian homes of material that was hard to censor and that would have been inconceivable a short time before. Films with explicit violence and sex, which no Christian would have gone out to see, appeared on the screen more or less 'accidentally' and were not switched off. Evangelicals were therefore more aware of secular thinking, but also more liable to be influenced by it. They could not easily live in an isolated cultural world.

It is noticeable that whereas before the war the majority of new converts came to faith in their teens, now many more were converted as students or later. Others started coming to church, or returned to it, after marriage. Often this was when children arrived, and the parents saw that moral teaching, and perhaps some religious faith to support it, was important in the prevailing moral chaos. This presented a fresh range of possibilities for outreach. In fact, the main outreach of many churches was no longer the Sunday services, but the mid-week activities. Here, the concerns that church members had in common with their neighbours and colleagues at work could be exploited in everything from groups for mothers and toddlers to those for pensioners. The rather few really good preachers, however, drew in many non-Christians and attracted young people. Even quite unexceptional preaching could build well on the personal 'friendship evangelism' of members if the services were intelligible.

Many Anglican churches abandoned the Prayer Book services except for communion and baptisms, and the other services then became almost indistinguishable from Free Church services. Anglican churches in Scotland, Ireland and Wales, however, were much more conservative than those in England. The Presbyterian churches were also more traditional, and the charismatic influences were less prominent there.

Some evangelicals, especially on the more charismatic wing of the movement, began to take less trouble about preparing their sermons than before. Certainly they were less determined to keep close to the real meaning of the passages they were expounding. If they were relying on the immediate inspiration of the Holy Spirit, that inspiration did not always seem to be given. Preaching could easily become predictable and repetitive. There was again, as there had been in the 1930s, a danger of alienating the more thoughtful young people, or at least leaving them with too little foundation for the battles of life. As one charismatic theologian expressed it later: 'It is relevant to reflect on the extent to which the charismatic movement may have contributed to the loss of biblical and theological literacy in the churches. If this is the case, then it is due, in part, to the way in which the experimental emphasis of the movement absorbs energy and attention which might otherwise be devoted to study and intellectual endeavour.'[3]

David Watson, Roger Forster and Michael Green became three of the best and most often used evangelists for church and student missions. The first two were emerging as definitely on the charismatic side and brought that influence into some new places. Interestingly, both were converted through the witness of their student CUs.

In this period there was an explosion of new evangelical songs, choruses and hymns. *Youth Praise* had appeared in 1966 (second enlarged edition 1969) and *Psalm Praise* in 1973. The overhead projector became a necessary piece of equipment in many evangelical churches. The older hymns were used much less, and the newer ones often (but by no means always) had less doctrinal content. Indeed, not a few could be sung with enthusiasm by New Age devotees. In these changes there were gains as well as losses. Some of the new songs were excellent and were easier for young people to use. Much depended on the selection, because some were empty, even if they had good tunes. Music groups and music directors were often given a fairly free hand, and sometimes had more influence than the ministers on the style and content of worship. For them, the music could be the first consideration, and they were not always theologically discerning. Many young people no longer knew what were regarded as the great evangelical hymns.

Ecumenical and denominational changes

Anglican–Methodist reunion had been discussed since 1955, and more publicly in the 1960s. The scheme was accepted by the Methodists but was turned down by the Church of England in 1969, 1971 and finally in 1972 by a narrow margin below the two-thirds majority required. This took place because a number of evangelicals, including J. I. Packer, worked with the Anglo-Catholics to defeat it. This highlighted the fact that, in order to limit the inroads of liberalism, evangelicals were working more with the high-church party.

In the middle of this debate, in 1970, Packer and Colin Buchanan combined with two prominent Anglo-Catholics to publish *Growing into Union*.[4] To many Free Church people this was a clear signal that Anglican evangelicals were moving into the mainstream of the Church of England and would find it impossible to maintain a distinctive biblical witness – a view hotly repudiated by Packer and others. But the agreements on episcopacy and baptism certainly encouraged that impression.

In 1977, a second National Evangelical Anglican Congress was held at Nottingham, as a follow-up to Keele ten years earlier. Raymond Turvey was again the Secretary, and John Stott the Chairman, as at Keele, but Stott's now frequent trips abroad had weakened his influence at home, and less conservative views began to be heard. Nottingham produced no new policies, but confirmed the emphases of Keele. It was stronger on infant baptism. One of the preliminary papers included the statement: 'The Church is, and must be, defined *sacramentally* by baptism . . . We could do worse therefore than use it as our working definition of the Church.' It spoke of 'the people gathered round their "bishop" ',[5] and in other ways indicated a very strong view of episcopacy. As a more conservative Anglican parson expressed it: 'The evangelical essentials were largely taken for granted at Nottingham, when it had become urgent for them to be reaffirmed, and concentration was almost entirely on other matters.'[6] This was a further blow to co-ordination of evangelical witness across the denominational divisions.

There were also danger signals appearing on the strictly theological front, which will be discussed below. There was often an assumption that sheer force of numbers would somehow shift the churches in an evangelical direction, when there was no strategy to ensure that they themselves remained solidly evangelical in the face of growing pressure from those with whom they sought to work. Also, the growing numerical strength was largely in percentage terms, while the actual numbers in the churches were declining. It was proper to seek to be the main representative voice of the churches, but it was much more important to ask if they were a growing proportion of the populace. If other sections of the churches were declining, it was no great gain if the evangelicals were not filling the vacuum. Being proportionately stronger is a cause for heart-searching as to how that position is being used, not a matter for self-congratulation. The fact that churches and Sunday schools were being closed (as they still are today) is a grievous sign of the loss of Christian background on which much evangelism depends. At least they taught the moral law, which is a fine foundation for the gospel and a cement for society.

In Scotland, the Crieff conferences, convened by William Still from 1970, became a focus for CE ministers in the Church of Scotland. They began to include some from Ireland and a very few from England. The brothers George and James Philip, who had been influenced by William Still when they studied in Aberdeen, emerged as leaders in important churches in university cities, and Eric Alexander at the Tron in Glasgow joined forces with the Crieff circle. In Wales, the Evangelical Movement of Wales conferences (in either Welsh or English) served a similar function.

Within the Baptist Union, Paul Beasley-Murray and others set up the Mainstream group in 1979.[7] This was partly a response to the 'Michael Taylor affair' in 1971. Michael Taylor, who was Principal of the Northern Baptist College, had given an address at the Baptist Union Assembly that year which seemed to call in question the full deity of Jesus Christ. The Baptist Union itself did not respond firmly, but a motion at the 1972 Assembly, affirming an orthodox Christology, was passed by about 1,800 to a mere 60 or 70 against.[8] This exposed the fact that whatever the official leadership of the Union and the colleges might believe, the Baptist churches were overwhelmingly more orthodox. That, and the hope of keeping the small but growing charismatic group together with the non-charismatic churches, encouraged the formation of Mainstream. It has never had a membership list, but a high proportion of younger ministers have been actively involved in its conferences from time to time, and it is still a focus for evangelical commitment.

These and other similar informal fellowships, such as the British Evangelical Council and the Fellowship of Independent Evangelical Churches (see chapter 4), provided much stimulus and encouragement to CE ministers or congregations that had lacked such support. Classical evangelicalism was spreading unobtrusively into a strong position in a growing number of local churches of all kinds.

At the same time, the Anglican enthusiasts for the Keele and Nottingham emphases continued to argue that they were recovering a biblical doctrine of the church. What they were in fact recovering was a renewed emphasis on the Church of England as the national church and of the local church as including at least all baptized people. The latter made church discipline virtually impossible. They seemed unaware of the fact that the number of people actually attending worship in Free Churches in England was almost equal to those attending the Church of England (it passed it in 1981).[9]

Theological trends

Nottingham was notable for two other things. David Watson, who was by now one of the leading Anglican charismatics, gave an address in which he made the remark: 'In many ways the Reformation was one of the greatest tragedies that ever happened to the church.' This was taken by many as signalling a recklessness in doctrine. Roman Catholics who shared the same experiences were welcomed on to the platform in some charismatic fellowships, though the Catholic authorities gradually drew them back into firmly RC activities if they could. In charismatic circles there seemed to be a danger of stressing experience at the expense of doctrine. The evangelical party in the Church of England emerged as 'less cohesive' doctrinally than it had been at Keele.[10]

A second new emphasis at Nottingham was on 'hermeneutics'. Anthony Thiselton, who had started by teaching at the BCMS college in Bristol and who was later to be Professor of Theology at Nottingham University, introduced the term to the congress. Because it was a novel term to most, it caused some ribald comments. It was, however, to prove significant in the next decades, especially in discussions about biblical ethics.[11] Hermeneutics was unfortunately used by some to avoid what had been taken as the plain teaching of the Bible on women's ministry, homosexual practice and other issues. This surfaced later. Despite the value of hermeneutics rightly applied, the idea spread that the teaching of the Bible was expressed in terms of the culture of its times to such an extent that it could not be related to life today as confidently as it had been. Hermeneutics thus became a tool for mischief as well as for good. As a term of abuse, the phrase 'proof-texting' began to be applied to anyone who used the actual words of the Bible to demonstrate a doctrine. A less clearly definable general sense of Scripture was invoked more often. It became less acceptable to say 'The Bible says'. A good deal of discussion of doctrine took flight from the actual words of Scripture and so became more the preserve of 'experts', that is, academic theologians, whose often unexamined philosophical presuppositions had much influence on their views. The Reformation principle of the perspicuity of the Bible was brought into doubt among the less conservative evangelicals, and a thorough examination of what was actually taught in a passage was less often the basis of teaching and preaching.

Two extremes of the theological spectrum grew in public attention in England during the 1970s, though they had less importance elsewhere. On the one hand the house churches, as they were usually called at that time, became a very substantial group of churches. They were divided into a number of networks, revolving round individuals or a small group of leaders. At that stage they were often very critical of the 'denominations', which they regarded as apostate or dead and bound for extinction as Christian forces. They attracted many young people to a charismatic style of worship and leadership, sometimes involving fairly authoritarian 'shepherding' of their members. As they became too big to meet in homes, they abandoned the title 'house churches' and became known more often as 'new churches'. Their essential elements were and have remained CE. The Bible is accepted as the final authority, but they give great importance to the more obviously supernatural gifts, such as tongues, prophecy and usually miraculous healings.

The charismatic emphasis has been somewhat lightly dismissed by some historians, such as David Bebbington,[12] as simply a manifestation in evangelical form of the counter-culture of the 1960s. To those concerned, however, it was a rediscovery of elements of primitive Christianity for which they found clear evidence in the Bible. If the cultural mood of the times helped people to see that, then (it was said) that did nothing to undermine their claims. Others, they felt, were bound by a different cultural bondage, so that they could not appreciate what was a valid understanding of the Scriptures. A charismatic emphasis became a much more normal part of evangelical church life in these years, both within the older churches and by secession outside them. Many congregations included a charismatic element, and the emphasis became far less divisive than it had been. This was partly because the more extreme groups tended to leave and form their own congregations, and partly because a charismatic element was more often accepted as a possible constituent of a broader fellowship, even by those who did not share its emphases. After a while it became necessary to control prophecies, and in many churches only those who were approved, or whose messages were first approved, were allowed to speak. Nevertheless, prophecies competed with Scripture, and often they were taken with the utmost seriousness as words from God in a way that had previously been reserved for the Bible. In some churches, prophecies were written down and circulated, and 'pictures' and prophecies were interpreted confidently as messages from God, becoming a major source of guidance, as in the Oxford Group/MRA. I will comment further on this development in the next chapter.

In the early 1970s, large numbers of young people from churches of all kinds attended Bible Weeks in the Dales and elsewhere to experience this kind of ministry. From 1979, Spring Harvest, with a mixture of charismatic and non-charismatic features, became a major youth event and introduced a more charismatic style of worship into some churches. Greenbelt – a 30,000-strong weekend of music and ministry – was started in 1974, with a strong charismatic element. Unlike Spring Harvest, it became wider than evangelical in its platform. Both of these get-togethers found that, in the midst of very relaxed, youth-orientated and charismatically influenced worship, there was a large demand for serious seminars on a wide range of social, ethical and apologetic issues. The programme was not all lightweight doctrinally, though the level at which these issues were discussed varied greatly.

At the other end of the theological spectrum, radically liberal theology came into greater prominence and was becoming more acceptable as a possible statement of a truly Christian view, making it more difficult for evangelicals in mixed denominations. Following the Michael Taylor debates, some churches left the Baptist Union, usually joining the FIEC. For parallel reasons, a few Anglican clergy, including Herbert Carson, resigned. Sidney Lawrence and Roland Lamb, who had been prominent in starting the Methodist Revival Fellowship, resigned from Methodism with David Pawson and others to join the independent sector.

In 1977, Don Cupitt, a radical Cambridge theologian, contributed with others to the book *The Myth of God Incarnate*.[13] Cupitt followed this up with high-profile broadcasts and television appearances under the title *The Sea of Faith*, explaining that he held very few of the traditional Christian beliefs but greatly valued the experience of conducting Anglican communion services. He followed this with *Taking Leave of God*[14] in 1980, which seemed to many to be almost atheism. Unlike at least one of the other authors of the first book, Cupitt did not resign his Anglican orders.

Radical theology was becoming more accepted as one option in the broad spectrum of Christian opinions. The idea that the churches stood for the great traditional doctrines of the faith became harder to maintain. While CEs made their position plain, it was harder to claim in the public arena that orthodox belief was the true Christian faith. The media did not, on the whole, find orthodoxy interesting, and gave their attention to heterodox views or the more photogenic aspects of the charismatic movement.

In the Presbyterian churches there were no high-profile radicals such as these, but the media, and to some extent the churches' own official pronouncements, tended to major on social and political questions. Much of the preaching was primarily ethical and rather vaguely devotional, without, as a rule, either attacking or teaching traditional doctrines. At the same time, liberal theology was giving fewer people a faith to live by. Churches without a 'converting ministry' were losing the vast majority of their young people by the age of sixteen.

By 1980, the high-church party in the Church of England had declined in influence and had no prominent theologians left. Professor Hastings described it as 'in disarray'. Their strength was in some parishes that approximated to the Roman Catholics, and in what was described as the 'liberal high-church' school that dominated Anglican university chaplaincies. The latter gave prominence to communion services, but were theologically vague. In general, the denominational chaplaincies tried to replace the SCM, which had almost collapsed. Very few of the university chaplains (usually full-time Anglican and Church of Scotland, and part-time Free Church) were evangelical, and certainly not CE. Considering their greatly superior facilities and staffing compared with the IVF's CUs, the strength of the CUs was a constant frustration to them.

As the proportion of the seventeen to twenty-one age group who were going into tertiary education was steadily increasing, the work among students was of growing importance to the churches. The teacher-training and technical colleges were left to the IVF, which changed its name in 1975 to the Universities and Colleges Christian Fellowship (UCCF) to recognize the fact that its work was now far wider than in the universities alone.

A straightforward biblical faith was proving far more effective than anything else in this section of the population. CU speakers were (and still are) expected to agree with the UCCF Doctrinal Basis, and committee members to sign it on taking office. There was a steady injection of CE influence into the church scene from this increasing source, though the lack of biblical background meant that it was not always in depth.

Social concern

The negative attitude to the social application of the faith among CEs had largely gone. There was generally, though not universally, an agreement that social concern and action were a part of the Christian's responsibility, and numerous conferences and consultations were held in the 1970s and 1980s, with reports and papers being published. John Stott's influential book *The Christian Mission in the Modern World* appeared in 1975.[15] As in other areas, Stott was a major influence on evangelical thinking on this topic. He was the greatest single influence in the Lausanne Congress in 1974, which, although it was titled the 'International Congress on World Evangelization', was to be most noted in many minds for its more positive emphasis on the place of social action as a partner with direct evangelism. Stott chaired the group that worded the Lausanne Covenant, which became an influential document worldwide.

What was usually lacking in the UK was any very effective way of putting this thinking into action. Not many evangelical churches got themselves deeply involved in meeting the needs of deprived areas in Britain, unless they were drawing their membership from those areas. Many city-centre churches drew their congregations largely from the suburbs, and very few evangelicals entered local or national politics. Evangelicals gave generously to TEAR Fund and responded to crisis appeals overseas, but were confused about the place of social action at home. Churches in deprived areas had the problem that those who were converted there often did better at their jobs and were promoted, rose up the social ladder, and then moved away for the sake of their children's education and other advantages. There were exceptions, but it was not easy. Tip-and-run evangelism was no adequate response. David Sheppard, a Cambridge graduate and All-England cricketer, had settled in the East End of London as Warden of the Mayflower Centre from 1958 to 1969, and provided a model for many who certainly admired his example but did not necessarily follow it. He had been converted at Cambridge through the CU and nurtured by the 'Bash Camps', so that he influenced a thoroughly conservative circle. When he became Bishop of Liverpool and published *Built as a City*[16] in 1974, he became a spokesman for evangelical involvement in inner-city work. The city missions and the Salvation Army had, of course, been involved all along, but Sheppard, who was a clear CE, set a stronger tradition of involvement in the structures that caused some of the problems. His partnership with the Roman Catholic Archbishop of Liverpool in these causes raised some eyebrows, but it was an example of the growing tradition of finding 'fellow belligerents' who might not agree on doctrine, but agreed on practical aims. The great evangelical social reformers of the nineteenth century had done the same, bringing together all people of good will to defeat the slave trade and other social evils, while they provided the main impetus.[17] Nevertheless, such co-operation was criticized by some of the more conservative, who felt that if that was the only way to make progress in social action, then it might be better to concentrate on purely evangelical philanthropy. There is still no consensus in evangelical circles about such co-operative efforts. Francis Schaeffer had been an advocate of working with 'co-belligerents' in practical issues on the basis of his well-thought-out theological approach.

The more pietistic evangelicals did not have the theological tools to develop a policy, and in addition there was much suspicion regarding the compromises that would be necessary in such co-operation over practical and ethical issues. Any co-operation on theological issues where there is important disagreement is quite another matter, but the two often become confused in people's minds. Evangelicals are not good at the compromises that are a necessary part of practical politics, because they tend to want to fight for a totally Christian solution and therefore often get nothing. The nineteenth-century reformers such as Wilberforce and Shaftesbury knew how to get something rather than nothing, and then how to build on that progressively, even though they were sometimes misunderstood as compromisers by their contemporaries. They also knew how to pitch their campaigns so as to win the support of many who would not be in agreement doctrinally.

In the 1930s, few evangelicals would have been willing to follow such a policy because they did not really recognize that, as Romans 2:14–15 states, non-Christians are not totally without an awareness of moral imperatives. They would have found it hard to acknowledge this, because they gave such prominence to the fact that our good deeds get us no nearer to heaven, and 'all our righteous acts are like filthy rags' (Is. 64:6). A stronger Reformational tradition now gave evangelicals a better basis for social action. In Reformed circles, Iain Murray's 1971 book *The Puritan Hope*[18] and W. Hendriksen's *More than Conquerors: An Interpretation of the Book of Revelation* served further to undermine the premillennial negative attitude to seeking to improve society.

There were some serious movements to try to influence society. In 1971 the Nationwide Festival of Light was launched, led by evangelicals, but including some others. This became the Care Trust, with a separate more political arm, Care Campaigns, in which O. R. Johnston played an important part as chief executive. There were other initiatives, including the influential founding by John Stott of the London Lectures in the 1970s, which led to the creation of the London Institute for Contemporary Christianity (LICC) in 1982. This became a sort of think-tank and training programme for evangelicals in this and a wide range of cultural, social and related areas. It was not the first such initiative. In 1969 the IVF had started the Shaftesbury Project as part of its graduate work, with its director as a member of IVF staff for the first three years, though it hoped to attract a circle wider than the graduate field and therefore intended to become independent. When it did so, it found difficulty in raising funds, and in 1988 it amalgamated with the LICC to create Christian Impact, which continues to have a worldwide ministry, since 1995 using the title Institute for Contemporary Christianity. In Northern Ireland, the Irish Christian Study Centre was started in 1977 by a group of lay people, led by some university lecturers.

In brief, there was a ferment of thought and activity in the 1970s, which started a good many fresh organizations. The magazine *Third Way* was started in 1977 and, with the IVF's magazine *The Christian Graduate* (later called *Christian Arena*), gave opportunity to discuss these and other issues in a critical way. There was little dispute that it was important to think out a biblical approach to social and political questions.

These discussions did, however, raise some troublesome theological questions, because some warm advocates of social action justified such action on a very flimsy biblical basis. If it was a straightforward attempt to meet social need, because the love of Christ must move us to do something, then there was no problem. The vast development of late nineteenth-century evangelical philanthropy, which was based simply on that motive, proved that it could be very effective. Evangelicals at that time did a great deal in direct action and, in contrast to the prevailing dependence on the draconian Poor Law, provided a philosophy of social action and structures that in many ways laid the foundations of the social services of today. Thomas Barnardo,[19] for instance, set an example in training children for useful employment. Of the thousands of these who were sent to Canada, only 2% reverted to crime, even though many of them had lived by stealing before he took them in (compare juvenile re-offending figures today!). Although such philanthropy was quite sophisticated in policy, it was unsophisticated in theology because no complex motives were needed.

When in this century social action was advocated on the basis of the doctrine of the kingdom of God, however, it opened up a series of disputes.

This was not only because liberal Christians had used this concept to promote unacceptable ideas of a 'social gospel' in the 1930s. Now it was coming in from different sources, especially from the South American writers on 'liberation theology'. Ronald Sider's *Rich Christians in an Age of Hunger*[20] appeared in the USA in 1977 (with an edited version in the UK in 1984) and had considerable impact. He and others following the same line seemed to have been over-influenced by liberation theology, because they argued that all actions for righteousness, even when done by total unbelievers (such as Marxists), were examples of 'kingdom activity'. Christopher Sugden raised some of these issues in his *Social Gospel or No Gospel?* in 1975, and John Stott attacked this standpoint in his debate with Sider in *Evangelism, Salvation and Social Justice*.[21] Although these were small Grove Booklets, they were read by many evangelical clergy. The debate unfortunately cast doubt in the minds of some regarding the justification of such activity, if indeed it needed such tenuous theological defence.

Meanwhile, John Stott and others were defending the duty of social action on a more secure basis, as for instance in Stott's *Walk in His Shoes*.[22] They insisted that the kingdom consists only of those who have been born again and that salvation categories do not belong to righteous deeds or relatively just structures of society, much as those things are to be appreciated and worked for as pleasing to God.

The Keele Statement on social concern ran: 'Christians share in God's work of mission by being present among non-Christians to live and to speak for Christ, and in His name to promote justice and meet human need in all its forms. Evangelism and compassionate concern belong together in the mission of God.'[23] The last sentence would surely command universal support among British evangelicals, even if some in North America might still question it. To be active in promoting justice would also have the support of almost all as, in many circumstances, a necessary way of meeting human need. So much is now agreed – at least in theory.

The Lausanne Covenant of 1974 included the statement: 'When people receive Christ they are born again into his kingdom and must seek not only to exhibit but also to spread its righteousness in the midst of an unrighteous world. The salvation we claim should be transforming us in the totality of our personal and social responsibilities. Faith without works is dead.'[24] This wording was the result of considerable debate, and a group of more radical evangelicals produced a supplementary paper giving considerably stronger emphasis to social action. The theological divide that emerged was between those who were beginning to describe all acts for social good (whether done by those within the kingdom or not) as a manifestation of the kingdom, and those who, while agreeing that social action for righteousness was a necessary result of being brought into the kingdom, held that on biblical grounds we should not use the term 'kingdom' to include righteous acts done by unbelievers.

This debate is not trivial, because, as the historian Brian Stanley shows,[25] the broader definition of the kingdom is in danger of drifting into the same position as the 'social gospel' of the last century, in which social action became synonymous with evangelism and those who do good with members of the kingdom. If this were to happen, it would be likely, as in the 1930s, to turn many evangelicals away from social action as something too closely identified with liberal theology. This would be a great loss, for it would encourage evangelicals to retreat into exclusively evangelistic activities, while a secular society is asking what are the obvious fruits of Christianity in society as well as in personal life.

Broadening the concept of the kingdom also has the initially surprising effect of *reducing* it to mere ethics. The teaching of Jesus on the kingdom cannot possibly be reduced to this. It is far more radical than that, though it has powerful ethical implications.

Whatever the outcome of these debates, the more immediate issue is whether evangelicals are going to act for social righteousness here in the UK. We may ask who today is notable for work to help the deprived – the homeless, the unemployed, single-parent families and other really poor people in the UK. In fact, it is still most often the unsophisticated, rather pietistic churches in run-down areas that are in on the action. Sir Fred Catherwood comments in his autobiography that when churches are so involved, they get a good hearing in the wastelands of inner cities.[26] Costly philanthropy continues in many mission halls and downtown churches, and is often unnoticed by those who discuss the theory. The All Souls Club House is still in action today, but few other well-to-do churches have similar activities.

Certainly we seem to be doing much less than our theologically less sophisticated nineteenth-century forebears did. There is no evidence that the nineteenth-century evangelicals were troubled by these theological questions.[27] They accepted a straightforward responsibility to help the deprived, and therefore set to work to tackle some of the structures that upheld such deprivation: for instance, prison reform, the slave trade, then slavery itself, labour laws, working conditions in certain industries and lack of educational facilities. Philanthropy of a personal kind was clearly not enough. The nearest that we have come in recent times to such a campaign is the 'Keep Sunday Special' campaign run by the Jubilee Centre, which had some political success for a time, and the Evangelical Alliance and the Care Trust in lobbying Parliament.

Talk about tackling unjust structures in the UK has so far produced very little, largely because there are too few Christians able and willing to give time to political activity. This situation is likely to continue until more suitably gifted Christians are encouraged to enter local politics, which is the usual path to national politics; and they will need very positive support from their churches if they are to persevere. Strong Christians, however, are commonly too busy in church responsibilities, and churches that gladly send one of their members abroad or into the ministry are rarely eager to encourage them into the equally tough world of political life. It was John Newton, the evangelical preacher and hymnwriter, who had to persuade Wilberforce not to go into the ministry, but to use his gifts in politics, to the great blessing of many and the honour of the gospel. Interestingly, when, later in life, Wilberforce published an evangelistic book, it had an enormous readership among non-Christians. He had won the right to be heard on the gospel and on many ethical issues. At the same time, Christians obviously have to use great discretion in their choice of political topics on which to speak, as painful experience in South Africa and Northern Ireland shows.

1980

By 1980 the clarity of the evangelical witness was beginning to be confused. The growth of the charismatic element (some of it seeing their special emphases as essential to gospel witness) and the loss of doctrinal substance in others who, while they valued their evangelical friends and their upbringing in CE circles, no longer stressed the characteristic CE doctrines, both contributed to loss of clear identity. Certainly CEs were less homogeneous than before. Where this represented greater specialization in the application of doctrine, it was usually a gain. Where it represented a change of central focus, it threatened serious weakness in those concerned. A growing self-confidence also seemed to contribute to this doctrinal carelessness.

At the same time, there were undoubted gains in the spreading out of the influence of biblical thinking into many areas of life, and these explorations offered the possibility of Christian influence in places where it was no longer being supplied by others. In a society that was rapidly becoming more secular, this was a challenge and an opportunity. The question was whether in developing in this way there would be a loss not merely of evangelical identity but also of doctrinal substance and clarity with which to tackle the opportunities.

7. ADJUSTING TO A
CHANGING SOCIETY:
1980–95

By 1980 the situation had changed from that of the 1960s in at least five important respects. It is harder to be sure of what is important in sketching more recent times, and others may detect different features, but, from my perspective, the following appear to be major changes.

Evangelicalism transformed

First, *evangelicals are more numerous* as a proportion of church life and to a lesser extent more numerous in absolute terms. The Evangelical Alliance, which includes evangelicals of all shades, often states that it represents a very large section of British Christianity. In some circles this has produced a not very modest, and potentially very damaging, triumphalism. 'God', we are warned, 'opposes the proud' (Jas. 4:6). That there has been an increase of numerical strength, however, there can be no doubt and most of it is in clearly CE circles. In a day of declining church membership, it is the evangelical churches that are not only in many cases growing, but (what is perhaps more significant) are often far more full of young people than others. That is not to deny that there are many small and struggling evangelical churches, especially in the countryside. A 1995 survey of churches in Wales reported that the growing churches were not only those with a ministry of biblical exposition but those whose members were reading the Bible for themselves.[1] In the universities, which in 1995 included a third of all people of the relevant age group, the evangelical CUs and the evangelical churches that attract students nearly always dominate the Christian scene, though the percentage of the student body that is involved is probably not often above 10%. The question is whether these and other young people are sufficiently well taught to stand firm and to grow as Christians in the world of work – or unemployment. An article by Dick Lucas[2] described the average CU member as zealous 'but clueless'. If that is sometimes true, it is because many of them are recent converts from a non-Christian background, and in any case few of them have been given much solid teaching in their churches. The same could be said of the members of the youth groups of many churches. This leaves them easily drawn away from biblical faith and practice, particularly when they go to jobs in areas without strong biblical churches.

Secondly, there is an alarming *deficit of biblical knowledge* among younger CEs and in the churches generally. Not everyone seems to realize how serious this loss is, and to do enough to try to remedy it by helping young Christians to develop regular personal prayer and Bible study, or to provide suitable materials to assist them in it. Without a revival of the 'quiet time' tradition (whatever it might be called today), it is easy to drift into a Sunday religion, with the weekdays left without spiritual input. Not all evangelical ministry aims to meet this need.

This has also created a growing gap between what preachers assume and what the hearers actually know. Evangelistic addresses often assume too much. The lack of any widespread conception of the holiness of God and his wrath against sin means that addresses that might have been well understood in the 1950s can seem largely irrelevant. Where Billy Graham is still seen as a model, it can mislead today if preachers move quickly to an appeal when hearers do not see why they need to respond. Evangelistic addresses sometimes contain very little gospel content. They call for a decision when people do not see that sin really matters. There is no 'fear of God' if he is seen as a sort of Father Christmas figure who ought to forgive everyone anyway and whose job is to make everyone happy. It follows that there is no astonished wonder at the grace of God. This loss of background knowledge makes both evangelism and Christian nurture harder. Both have to start further back, and can assume very little. Those brought up in a strong Christian tradition often fail to understand this, so that their evangelistic approaches can miss the mark. Apologetics also has to change its targets to some extent. There is less thought-out opposition than in the 1930s and a more widespread assumption that Christianity is irrelevant.

The task of giving young Christians a strong biblical foundation is more difficult today where they do not know the Bible, did not learn it at school, and, even if they attended Sunday school or a church youth group, did not always get much there. The influence of television has driven much evangelical youth work into trying to imitate its methods, which are always more concerned with entertainment and very short snatches of information or mood than with serious learning. Worship leaders easily perform like chat-show hosts rather than spokespersons for God. A load of humour makes it very difficult to turn to thinking of the gospel as a serious matter. Fearful of seeming dull in an age when to be 'boring' is thought of as the greatest offence, it is not easy to know how to teach well and hold the attention of any but the more academic young people – though the attention span is frequently underestimated, as good schoolteachers know. Those speaking to children frequently give amusing talks with a soon-forgotten verse of the Bible tacked on at the end to make some Christian point. The illustrations are then remembered without knowing what they illustrated. Even telling Bible stories seems to be a forgotten art, and who does not love a good story? The result is that some youth services end up with very little biblical content. There are no easy solutions, but the situation is more difficult than it was, particularly for young people growing up in a world where there is little acknowledgment even of the law of God, let alone of the truths of the gospel.

A third feature of the scene is the growth of the *Pentecostal denominations and other charismatic churches*, some of them large and effective in outreach and some inward-looking. They see conversions, and also attract people from other churches (partly because there is today very little loyalty to any denomination). Therefore many people attend a charismatic church for a while and then change, and *vice versa*. Generally, charismatic churches tend not to give such thorough teaching as in the mainline evangelical churches, though there are exceptions. While some charismatic leaders scorn doctrinal depth, others see the need for more of it. The songs that are chosen represent this. If one compares them with the hymns of Charles Wesley, written, it is worth noting, in the midst of a major revival, the contrast is stark. Presumably Wesley was setting out to teach through what people sang, as well as to give voice to praise. In an age of biblical illiteracy, it is important that the songs that people will remember and sing to themselves, perhaps for a lifetime, convey truth and not merely moods. If songs are thought of more as a way of self-expression than of praising God for one or more of the very good reasons that we have for praise, they will reinforce the subjective and human-centred trend of our culture and fail to help much in the long run. We could compare the Psalms, with their 'I love the Lord *because* . . .' Most of them give their reasons for praise, so that to sing just the first or last verses is to miss the point.

In the 1990s the 'Toronto blessing' arrived in the UK, and carried some evangelicals further away from rational and doctrinal substance in church life. At least one of its prominent advocates is quoted as saying, 'Feel, don't think', and 'If it makes sense it's not from God – if it is from God it doesn't make sense.'[3] This is no doubt an extreme point of what is an extreme aspect of the charismatic movement in the 1990s (the movement itself is divided over Toronto), but it indicates the fact that there is in that movement such a stress on experience that it can easily become anti-doctrinal and effectively anti-rational again. The history of the Quakers and of the Oxford Group/MRA in particular is a warning. Doctrine is sometimes being treated as the opponent of true spiritual experience. Yet without doctrine (that is, revealed truth), people are left open to all the vagaries of New Age spirituality and other cultural pressures, as when (for instance) it is proposed that we return to Celtic spirituality and put its symbolism above doctrine. There are signs that even some of the leaders in charismatic churches are easily vulnerable to ideas contrary to biblical teaching, as shown by some recent writings under titles such as *The Post-Evangelical*[4] by a former house-church leader, and *The Radical Evangelical* by a Baptist charismatic spokesperson, the latter now seeming to be typically LE.[5]

It is too early to be able to say how the charismatic churches will develop. Meanwhile, in many mainstream denominational and independent churches, there are charismatics who have learned to work harmoniously alongside others for a united witness. Only if the particular emphases of the charismatic movement are held to be an essential part of gospel witness, however, does such co-operation become almost impossible, and then those concerned usually withdraw into a separate church.

Fourthly, the 1990s generation is *not inclined to be committed to anything long-term*, either in planning their future careers or in their friendships. This rubs off on Christians. Thus short-term Christian service is popular. Although that does sometimes lead on to long-term service, to be committed to long-term missionary work or Christian ministry (for instance) is less compelling. Marriage vows are no longer seen by many non-Christians as binding, and this attitude to commitment and loyalty easily lingers in the thinking of those converted from a culture where such a mindset rules. The older attitudes (represented, for instance, by the missionary challenge at Keswick) are easily replaced by the current search for the feel-good factor or for fulfilment. At work, people ask themselves whether they are finding satisfaction or fulfilment in their job, not whether they are making a good contribution to their employer, customers or society. In their marriages they look for personal satisfaction, and do not wonder whether they are giving as much as they could in love. In conversion they really desire a new ego-trip rather than a new relationship with God.

In this context, the 'health and wealth' or 'prosperity' gospel is attractive, though thankfully less so in the UK than in the USA. A recent video for churches on guidance for young people emphasized thinking about what they would *like* to do, what would give them adequate *money*, and what they might *succeed* in. It failed to mention the Christian ideal of service that has been the foundation of a Christian idea of work until recently, especially in the professions. The example of Jesus in washing his disciples' feet, and the challenge to make sacrifices, are not popular today. The aim of finding satisfaction or fulfilment inevitably leads to instability, or at best dissatisfaction, as no-one is 100% fulfilled for long in this imperfect world.

Fifthly, the intellectual shift that is called *postmodernism* has infiltrated church life. In so far as it represents disillusionment with the Enlightenment tradition now called 'modernism', it has some positive features – even if many see it as simply the endpoint of the modernist tradition. In general, however, it is against any idea of truth or right and wrong as other than a statement of personal preference.[6] Facing this cultural change, the churches have to be determined in declaring their message as a timeless word from God. If they fail to be clear here, they are regarded as stating just one point of view in a pluralistic world. Here all religions are merely a matter of how *we* see things. Just as in the first century, when the Christian faith ran contrary to the prevailing cultural pluralism (as Paul found at Athens), so today, Christians need to confront many aspects of current culture and leave the result to God. In practice, it looks as if such a bold stand is the most effective, as it was then. To go half way to meet the errors of the culture is not to help people, and leads constantly into compromise. The cynical question 'What is truth?', being asked again today, does not have a good pedigree! It enabled Pilate to crucify Jesus when he knew him to be innocent.

Much of the anti-doctrinal emphasis mentioned above can be traced to this postmodern culture, which is particularly seductive to those who watch a great deal of television, where it predominates today. It is different from, and in some ways more dangerous than, the anti-intellectualism of the 1930s, for the latter was largely a defence mechanism on the part of those who did not have the theological tools to grapple with rival views. Today's antipathy to doctrine easily becomes a vehicle for extravagant claims to authoritative personal revelations that would not stand up to careful criticism. It also undermines any attempt to obey the command to love God with all our minds. It can make worship vacuous if the revealed character of God (his 'name') is not understood and made its basis. Yet many church members have the most vague grasp of doctrine and do not see how it inspires worship and controls action.

The hermeneutical debate bears on this issue. In literature studies and in other disciplines, postmodern views demand a retreat from belief not only in objective truth but also from any secure understanding of the meaning of a text. The extreme 'deconstruction' school is only beginning seriously to penetrate theological circles, but the programme of always questioning the accepted meaning of a piece of writing is growing in influence. These ideas are obviously attractive to liberals, and evangelical Christians have yet to develop an adequate apologetic here. Evangelicals do believe that the Bible conveys truth in such a way that we can be sure of at least its necessary elements, and a few writers have begun to address the issues.[7]

Evangelical parties?

When CEs have been deprived of fellowship with like-minded people, it has repeatedly resulted in their being absorbed into the general outlook of their denomination and ceasing to have a very clear witness to the great truths that classical evangelicalism seeks to maintain as essential biblical Christianity. This steady erosion of the doctrinal clarity of evangelical witness has become more dangerous as the general outlook of their denominations has become increasingly vague. If in particular denominations there is no defined evangelical party, then informal fellowships are vital to many young ministers and lay leaders. For a while after the war, the IVF, with its Graduates' Fellowship and its literature, provided such a fellowship to many. Since then the Westminster Fellowship, the Fellowship of Independent Evangelical Churches, the Eclectics in the Church of England, the Methodist and Baptist Revival Fellowships, the development that created the Evangelical Movement of Wales and more recently the Crieff Fellowship in the Church of Scotland have done the same. Where there is resistance to the idea of a 'party' within a church (as there is particularly in Presbyterianism), and where evangelicals have been promoted in the Anglican churches, many who were regarded as clear CEs have appeared to be moving into a more broadly 'Christian' but not clearly evangelical position, and have felt that they must no longer be distinctive in their own stance. They have then often raised no objections to what are in their view erroneous opinions. They have ceased to 'contend for the faith'.

In *Scotland*, Rutherford House was created in 1983 as a centre for research and study on a strongly conservative basis, and the Scottish Evangelical Theological Society, with its conferences and journal, has included those of several denominations. The Bible Training Institute in Glasgow has upgraded its courses, changed its name to Glasgow Bible College and obtained validation for its own degrees in theology since 1992 – the first such degree independent of the universities in Scotland in living memory. The Scottish Baptist College and the denomination, though small, are now almost totally CE. Meanwhile, the Highland Theological Institute has been formed in Elgin to provide CE theological education up to degree standard. The great loyalty to the denomination within the Church of Scotland has had its virtues, but there are now more evangelicals who wonder whether the price has been too high in failure to produce a distinctive CE witness that can distance itself from the more liberal, or merely vague, consensus. More and more people do want to know what is the Christian message for today, and mere ethics is not enough. A small but distinct group of evangelicals has emerged in the Scottish Episcopal Church, to the surprise of some who had regarded it as totally in the high-church tradition.

In *Wales*, the Evangelical Movement of Wales, with its publishing house, has become a coherent CE fellowship. The Evangelical Theological College of Wales at Bridgend, which it created, is now a considerable college, with a good number of postgraduate students in addition to people training for the ministry at home and abroad. Degrees are validated by the University of Glamorgan, and in 1995 they graduated their first PhD.

In *Ireland*, the Presbyterian and Anglican causes remain very mixed. After a phase in which Anglican CE leadership passed in considerable measure to laymen and the informal counsel of some older ministers, a group of younger ministers has emerged to build up large congregations. Fellowship with other CE churches and across denominational boundaries has continued in the work of SU, the UCCF and the CE missionary societies such as OMF and BCMS (now renamed Crosslinks), which latter has been important in the Church of Ireland. The population is small enough for much informal fellowship to flourish without too much organization. Ministerial training (apart from among the Baptists, who are a consistently CE group) is still largely, but no longer entirely, in the hands of people of less than CE convictions, though the strength of grassroots evangelicalism in the Presbyterian Church in Ireland is ensuring some CE appointments and is likely to do more in the future. Very few CEs in the less democratic Church of Ireland have been promoted to positions of official influence, and ordinands have been going to English evangelical colleges such as Oak Hill whenever possible. In neither church is there a distinct evangelical party, or a distinct party of any doctrinal kind, as in the Church of England.

The political conflicts have confused church life in many cases, as ministers not infrequently have strong political affiliations and those who try to create conditions for reconciliation are not always welcomed in the mainline churches. Both the two high-profile 'reconciliation communities' in Ulster, at Corrymeela and Rostrevor, are, however, led by CEs. The Troubles erupted just as evangelicals were finding an open door into Catholic circles, and it is now much more difficult to reach Catholics, except for some who have been influenced by the charismatic movement. Interestingly, Herbert Carson, who returned to Ulster in 1967 as a Baptist minister, and had written trenchantly in criticism of Catholic theology, found many openings to talk and debate with Catholics, as the clarity of his criticisms seemed to be more appreciated than polite nothings would have been.

When in 1985 the British Council of Churches sent a mainly English deputation to Ireland to investigate the situation as regards evangelism, they reported that 'In marked contrast to England, there is in Ireland a common religious awareness. Much evangelism can presuppose knowledge about Christianity and an accepted moral framework. Traditional forms of evangelism remain acceptable [with] many local missions and evangelistic services, with a much greater response ratio than would be expected in England.'[8]

In *England*, the evangelical community became increasingly diverse in the 1980s and early 1990s. Some of this was a not unhealthy result of specialization. Some evangelicals were deeply involved in inner-city work, for instance, or youth evangelism, or politics or apologetics. Inevitably they did not always fully appreciate the emphases of others with priorities different from their own. Diversity around an agreed doctrinal position in essentials is no bad thing. In the end it is doctrine that determines practice, and there are yet fresh applications of biblical truth to be explored.

The chief factor that worried some observers including myself, however, was that there was a growing doctrinal diversity, and that this concerned not only the more problematic aspects of doctrine (such as limited atonement, on which evangelicals had never been agreed). It often concerned quite basic truths such as the substitutionary nature of the atonement, whether there is salvation apart from the work of Christ, and, more generally, the nature of the authority of the

Bible. Leadership was no longer so exclusively in the hands of conservatives. A new liberal evangelicalism has clearly emerged, though those concerned usually do not like the title and prefer to be called 'open evangelicals'. This puts them alongside others of a conservative theology who only wish to stress their independence of mere evangelical traditions by using the same title. In addition, in the name of hermeneutics, the ethical teaching of the apostles (as traditionally understood) on such matters as church order, male–female relationships in the home and the church, and more recently on homosexual practice, is set aside by some and treated as merely the first-century expression of practical policies that we can apply quite differently today.

In this situation, the Evangelical Alliance has gained in importance and in public profile, encompassing a wide range of evangelicals, including the large and important Pentecostal denominations. As mentioned earlier, it was created (in 1846) to bring together evangelicals from many churches, at a time when denominational boundaries were strong and the distinctives of evangelicalism could be defined easily. Today it aims to include all evangelicals, and has been successful in bringing in very many independent groups with their own special agendas. An unfortunate result is that the term 'evangelical' is used fairly loosely (as is shown by the fact that the volume written to celebrate its 150 years of existence emphasizes some of the divisions in evangelicalism but does not even mention that the Alliance has always had a Doctrinal Basis).[9] As with all groupings, unless some doctrinal parameters are defined, the term 'evangelical' will soon mean very little, as the drift of the LEs in a previous generation illustrates. It would be better to reaffirm what constitutes classical evangelicalism, as I have attempted in chapter 1, and leave people to state the ways in which they either depart from it or add to it, qualifying it by terms such as 'liberal' or 'charismatic', or in other ways that represent their priorities.

In the Church of England debates over the full ordination of women, evangelicals were not united. The measure was passed only in 1992, when a fair number of less conservative evangelicals supported it, arguing in some cases that the biblical idea of headship, and the specific passages such as 1 Timothy 2:11–15 and Ephesians 5:25–33, either were not intended to be for all time or could be understood as largely irrelevant today. Some very strained exegesis is involved in many cases. That discussion was complex, because Anglo-Catholics and evangelicals had totally different reasons for opposing it. The fact that the Anglo-Catholics opposed it because they did not believe that a woman could offer the mass carried absolutely no weight with evangelicals, and even encouraged some of them to support the ordination of women. The evangelicals were happy for any suitably authorized person to lead a communion service, and began to argue for lay people to do so. The CEs were concerned about who had the ultimate teaching and disciplinary role, but many less conservative evangelicals were increasingly handing over that role to academic theologians, away from bishops or pastors. As I discuss below, this has far-reaching implications, because the academic world is in many ways inhospitable to a biblical theology and liable to passing fashions, as the changing kinds of issues that dominated theology this century demonstrate.

The Reform tradition

Almost all evangelical Anglicans had agreed the Keele Statement in 1967. But at the third National Evangelical Anglican gathering in 1988, held at Caister and called a 'Celebration', not a Congress, one group was left in considerable disquiet at the way things were going. They perceived a growing liberalization of the evangelical community and a carelessness about doctrine that threatened to undermine evangelical witness. Such people created the Proclamation Trust (which was based on St Helen's, Bishopsgate, in London, where Dick Lucas is the Rector) and the Anglican group Reform.

The Reform group in the Church of England was created in 1993 in the aftermath of the decision by the Synod in 1992 to ordain women to the priesthood. Its origins go back further, and it represented those who were very unhappy about the growth of liberalism in high places in the Church of England and the failure of the bishops to do anything about it. The talk at Nottingham about people 'gathering round their bishops' in unity seemed to them nonsensical in view of the radical theology of people like the then Bishop of Durham, David Jenkins. By 1995 there was discussion about the ordination of practising homosexuals and lesbians and, while the bishops did not accept such a move, they appeared to tolerate these practices among lay people, and at least one bishop said that he might ordain such people. That was the last straw for Reform, which talked of setting up some form of support system as an alternative to the normal archdeacons and bishops. If this was attacked as becoming 'a church within a church', it had a precedent in the Eclectics set up by John Stott in the 1950s. The call at Keele to become fully involved in the Church of England 'at all levels' was no longer an agreed position for the more conservative evangelicals. At a time in which the denominations no longer adhere to their confessional statements and allow all sorts of unbiblical views to be voiced, anyone who stands out for classical evangelicalism is easily made to seem eccentric or disruptive of the happy but now largely vacuous unity of their denomination.

The fact is that, as with the liberals of the past, once serious doubt is cast on doctrinal certainties it will not be long before the same uncertainty applies to ethics. At issue is not merely the perspicuity of the Bible, but the authority of the apostles for all time. In the 1995 symposium with the significant title *Has Keele Failed?*,[10] the author chosen to reply to Reform was a curate, Peter Barron. He attacks the Reform group for being too strong on substitutionary atonement and the perspicuity of Scripture and for not having given way to the trends of postmodernism. The points he is making are typical of the LEs of the Anglican Evangelical Group Movement in the 1930s, who regarded the CE position as hopelessly out of touch with modern thought. That particular author may be extreme in the vehemence with which he attacks traditional evangelical orthodoxy. He and others, however, frequently caricature those older positions, describe Reform as a retreat into a ghetto, and speak as if what they themselves are saying is somehow novel and daring, when it is merely a repetition of the 1920s departure of the LEs from biblical orthodoxy. Similar positions are being taken by others from both Anglican and Free Church standpoints.

There was at the same time a group of younger CE Free Church leaders who took a fresh initiative to rebuild fellowship and co-operation with the more conservative Anglicans. The Proclamation Trust quickly included non-Anglicans, and when it set up a one-year training course as a preparation for ministry, its Director was David Jackman, who moved from being the Minister at Above Bar Church, Southampton – one of the largest Free Church congregations in Britain. The Proclamation Trust conferences for preachers attract people of all kinds of church affiliation, and have become a major meeting-place for CE ministers across the denominational boundaries and a positive force for strong expository preaching.

Of course, history never repeats itself exactly. The CE positions are in many ways far stronger today than those of the 1930s. Many have a good ministry in depth and encourage their members to think through the application of the faith in an open and encouraging way that would have been rare in the 1930s. At the same time, a superficial ministry is all too common. People then complain that the sermons are predictable and repetitive and do not satisfy or strengthen the rising generation. CEs, however, have a respectable intellectual and theological leadership and literature today. It may not be outstanding, but it is as good as any other section of the churches. CEs are also more open-minded in a way that was rare in the 1930s. They are able to look critically at all kinds of issues, as is exemplified by a book such as John Stott's *Issues Facing Christians Today* (1984).[11] If CEs seem reactionary to others, it is partly, just as Peter Barron states, that they are not giving way to the secular culture, with its denial that any truths are absolute, or that anything is good or evil for all time.

A new liberal evangelicalism

The division between classical evangelicals and the newly developing liberal evangelicals is again sharpening and will not be easy to heal. Indeed, it is probably best that it should be affirmed rather than obscured. Either (for instance) substitutionary atonement is, or is not, a vital element in biblical teaching. If it is not, it is unclear how people can be led to a proper assurance of salvation or to the New Testament kind of wonder and worship of the God of grace. Even more fundamentally, either the Bible is, or is not, the unique and final authority in all matters of faith and conduct. 'Open evangelicals' are mostly anxious to avoid any repetition of the disastrous drift of the LEs in the 1930s and 1940s, but they are going to be preserved from it only by a strongly renewed emphasis on the final and sufficient authority of the Bible, on biblical doctrine, and on good biblical exposition. Otherwise they will have too little doctrine to apply to today's world and its thought.

A new polarization into CE and LE groups, with little or no fellowship between them, would be to leave the open evangelicals to drift away from classical positions just when they need encouragement to stay true to the biblical witness. A too strident and aggressive CE stance will drive others away from its orthodoxy as it sometimes did in the 1930s, and a too dismissive LE stance will mean that others give them up as hopeless. As in the 1940s, a recovery of solid biblical doctrine could restore unity and stability. There will not be unity in merely calling themselves 'evangelicals', without some clear emphasis on agreed doctrine, in a spirit of humble dependence on the Bible and a willingness to be corrected by a better understanding of it.

If it is asked how a new liberal evangelicalism has developed, when in the 1960s it seemed that the CEs were overwhelmingly dominant and likely to remain so, I believe the answer is twofold. First, as in the 1930s, many evangelicals do not have enough biblical doctrine in their thinking to resist the pressures of our culture when they, very honourably, seek to witness within it. They easily lose the control of their thinking that the Bible should give. Secondly, again as in the 1930s, theological education has undermined the faith of many, as I discuss below.

The present situation

The evangelical community therefore finds itself numerically stronger, better equipped to grapple with intellectual, apologetic, ethical, cultural and social issues, but more diverse than in the 1950s and 1960s. Among other groupings, it now includes a large charismatic community and a developing LE tendency. Carelessness about doctrine seems to be on the increase as the subjective emphasis of the prevailing culture infiltrates into church life, and a renewed anti-doctrinal streak emerges in some circles. We cannot, however, avoid the fact that the Bible is full of doctrine. It is true that it is not academic theology in the modern mode, but it is deep and moving revelation of truths that the largely uneducated early churches were expected to be able to grasp and enjoy. When an elder of an evangelical church confessed to me that he found the New Testament letters too difficult, I was alarmed. The gospels and the Old Testament are also full of meaty doctrine.

What has given doctrine a bad image in some circles is either its use as a merely intellectual debating exercise or its aridity when separated from the heartwarming worship and obedience of the God of truth and grace. It is striking that the New Testament letters repeatedly move from a more doctrinal opening section to a more practical one through an appeal to have a new 'mind'. Romans 12:1–2, for instance, appeals to us, in view of God's mercy (which Paul has taken eleven chapters to explain), to offer our bodies as living sacrifices, which is our 'spiritual act of worship', and to 'be transformed by the renewing of [our] *mind*'. Having a Christian mind is not an optional extra for the learned; it is to have our outlook transformed by the biblical revelation, and much of that is doctrine. It will not just drop into our psyche without a grasp of God's truth given by the Holy Spirit in the Bible. Those who stress that the mind is affected by sin and that it is not reliable (which is true) need to be reminded that it is the heart that is described as 'deceitful above all things and beyond cure' (Je. 17:9). To escape from the mind to the heart is not to go to any safer ground. Anti-intellectualism and an anti-doctrinal stance are emphatically not what the Bible requires of us, and their dangers are evident today, as they have been in past history when people rely on what they *feel* is right.

There is, no doubt, a complex of causes of the present lack of cohesion of evangelicalism, but the paramount one must be the weakness of biblical foundations. This has arisen where there is either compromise with the current culture or the plain failure of biblical education. On this last point, at the elementary level, there are weaknesses in the teaching that the youngest church members have received. At the academic level, the recent style of theological education for ministers and other church leaders deserves more examination. While liberalism has failed at the grass-roots level, there are reasons why it still has powerful advocates at the level of academic theology. It therefore constantly re-invades the local churches and, where it rules, reduces their ministry to merely human opinion.

Evangelical theological education

One of the most important lessons of the period before the war is that no-one can afford to neglect theological education. A conservative and doctrinally strong evangelical theology was resurrected by the CEs in the 1940s, and established in the 1950s and 1960s as the dominant evangelical theology. In that time it was recovered without the help of the academic theological community and in the face of its opposition.

Up to the 1970s, Tyndale House and the Tyndale Fellowship were almost the only evangelical attempts to do battle at an academic level. Donald Wiseman[12] always stressed that while it was impossible for the House to become expert in all aspects of theology, it should and could become the best residential library for biblical studies (in the sense of Old Testament, New Testament and biblical archaeology). Its aim to attract scholars from all over the world has been notably achieved, serving to build up an international fellowship of like-minded academics.

This, however, left a relative weakness in doctrine and ethics, which needed to be remedied. In 1987, the UCCF launched the Whitefield Institute in Oxford to try to train up people in systematic, biblical and philosophical theology and ethics as well as religious education. The need for this was well illustrated when in 1985 David Jenkins, then Bishop of Durham, published his doubts about the bodily resurrection of Christ and his virgin birth. The Warden of Tyndale House, Murray Harris, produced an excellent riposte, arguing convincingly that it was not possible to understand the biblical material in the way that Jenkins attempted to do.[13] The reply, however, was that even if the biblical writers did think like that, we do not do so now in a post-Kantian age; the philosophical shift makes the New Testament position untenable today. The evangelical community appeared to have no-one with the necessary weight, and inclination, to make a response at that level. We need devout evangelical scholars in all fields.

If the assumptions and methodology of the academic theological community are still in many ways liberal in the 1990s, there are some encouragements in that there are already more people of a relatively orthodox position gaining teaching posts in universities and colleges. The often unspoken presuppositions of the university faculties, however, remain in many ways inhospitable to an evangelical theology, as is explored below.

Meanwhile, the denominational colleges (including Pentecostal institutions such as Mattersey Hall) and most of the Bible colleges are now working up to degree standard, and have a growing student body with a number of postgraduates. London Bible College, which had grown quickly to 100 students by 1953, now has over 300 full-time students, making it one of the largest theological training establishments in Britain. College lecturers mostly have PhDs and are up to date in their reading, though one has to admit that some lecturers in the 1950s, when PhDs were rare, were just as well qualified, and sometimes better qualified, for the task. Often they were nearer to the proper priorities for ministerial training. The colleges, however, face many of the same problems as the faculties, especially where they try to follow the universities' agenda.

First, in order to qualify as accepted scholars and to get their students through exams, they have, at least in the recent past, been drawn into using the tools and adopting the tradition and the methodology of university theology. The pressure is less now that the colleges have their own degrees, validated by universities, but the tradition remains. University theology in the twentieth century has been both highly reductionist and also very rationalistic. Its reductionism means that there is very little scope for an overall biblical theology. Outside Scotland, there was until recently very little teaching of either systematic theology or (even less) biblical theology. Few teachers apart from CEs still believe that there is a consistent biblical theology. Academic scholars delight to find differences between the various authors, and, if possible, between an author's earlier and later writings. (How else can one find something original to say for a thesis?) The Bible is then treated as bits and pieces of a mosaic that do not fit together. It also means that by concentrating on language, theologians are free to impose their own presuppositions, whether they are biblical or not, and doctrines that require thinking at a more synthetic level than that of particular texts tend to be sidelined.

Reductionism also means that, ignoring the spiritual message, we are told to treat the Bible as any other book (which evangelicals at least know is a misleading part-truth). Then the rationalism[14] of such studies is understandable, especially when the standard of criticism is not to treat it like living literature but, as is sometimes said, 'scientifically'. The modernist tradition, in which scientific knowledge is an ideal, still rules in much university theology, even when modernism no longer rules in many other arts faculties. Theological study has been highly rationalistic, and this has produced a tradition of believing only what can be rationally justified. Evangelicals working in this milieu have followed the tradition and argued for a conservative position on exclusively rational grounds. They have been pushed into this policy by the desire to defend biblical teaching in the only way that others will accept. Those great doctrines that are more difficult to defend in this way, but are a matter of plain revelation (such as the second coming of Christ, an objective atonement, and final judgment), are frequently questioned, marginalized as far as our present faith is concerned, or regarded as merely an interesting ancient belief.[15]

Secondly, to show that our Lord and the apostles taught something is no longer regarded as sufficient. It is hard to set out an unambiguously revealed theology and to speak of a word from God. As John Wenham expressed it, the result is that people end up as conservative liberals rather than slightly liberal conservatives. They have accepted the liberal methodology, and its consequences emerge only later in their ministry. Thus even F. F. Bruce, who had done so much to revive evangelical scholarship, eventually came to hold that the apostle Paul was in error on at least one major point.[16] Bruce was above all a linguist and did not seem to see the doctrinal implications of this position. The rationalistic tradition, accepted in much evangelical apologetics for an orthodox faith, seems to explain at least in part the ease with which some who have been strongly conservative shift from those moorings when confronted by scholarship of a liberal tradition. Having worked for so long in a rationalistic tradition, it is easy to move on to *believing* only what can be easily justified in that tradition.

Thirdly, theology has become divorced from both ministry and spiritual life. Lectures are very rarely heartwarming, leading naturally into praise and worship, as both our Lord's teaching and the New Testament letters do. Some people are therefore opting for no professional theological training, looking only for some guided reading while in active ministry. Since even that reading easily gets squeezed out, it is easy to lose doctrinal depth and the benefits of the mutual criticisms of a student community. Nevertheless, some of the best preachers (by no means most) are almost without formal theological training, which suggests that a larger element of training 'on the job' may be needed – as is increasingly being recognized in medicine. Evangelical preachers are often frustrated by commentaries that spend so much time discussing unorthodox views, many of which really do not need to be taken seriously, that they despair of getting a lot of help from them. They easily stop reading widely, or look to older, more doctrinally minded writers whose works, however, are harder to relate to the questions of today.

Finally, reductionism means that developing an overall biblical theology is very hard work. This is aggravated by the effect of a PhD training. Working for a PhD gives a good training in critical thinking, but it has taught people to concentrate on details and they finish by treating some small portion of the Bible, or area of doctrine or ethics, in isolation. Theses with a wide theological scope are rare. The PhD mentality is hard to escape. Some students, even in evangelical colleges, therefore complain that they are given numerous opinions on every text or subject, but little help in developing an overall framework within which to set the different views. This leaves them having to supply that framework themselves, if they have the ability to do so. It also opens the door to uncertainty about issues that were regarded as certain in an evangelical theology a short time ago, especially in an age that dislikes certainty. Students are expected to develop a consistent position when their teachers either do not have one or fear to present it if they have.

As a result, by no means everyone is a better pastor and preacher for all the theological education today. There is little ability to present the message as a word from God, and sermons are full of 'I think . . .' as if that were of any real importance. As a student worker expressed it recently, today we have not only to *be* biblical in what we teach but also to *demonstrate* that what we teach comes out of the Bible. It is related of Professor Adolf Schlatter that, when congratulated by a foreigner on being almost the only German theologian left who 'took his stand firmly on the Bible', he replied, 'On the contrary, I sit under the Bible.' He was rightly distinguishing between a mere formal principle that can be held with pride, and a humble biblical faith that will try to hold and respond to what it is given.

We do not seem generally to have recovered a consistently evangelical way of doing and teaching theology, and some of those who are looked to for theological leadership disappoint. When London Bible College started preparing its students for the London University external BD, Martyn Lloyd-Jones sounded an alarm and lost interest in the college that he had helped to create. That London BD syllabus was admittedly much more destructive than many today, but the college felt that to get grants for their students and to get its graduates into Baptist Union churches, they needed such a qualification. In 1977, Lloyd-Jones led the way in setting up the London Theological

Seminary[17] to try to do better, and now there is a group of independent Bible colleges and other institutions seeking for a more pastorally relevant way than the university tradition. How successful these will be remains to be seen. Meanwhile, the main denominations often require their ordinands to take their own courses in addition to any previous training they may have had elsewhere. The independent churches, which are now the main evangelical presence in some large towns, do not have the same restrictions. If this means a break with the traditions of the university theology faculties, so be it. Christianity has always been a matter of divine revelation rather than what can be argued for by human reason. No university in Britain would now boast that for them 'the fear of the Lord is the beginning of wisdom'. One wonders if any university theology department could rightly lay claim to that motto today. Training for ministry surely ought to do so, and not to ape the university faculties, which have increasingly different aims and intellectual foundations.

If the Bible colleges and evangelical theological colleges are able to develop a new kind of learned theological education that is at once biblical, doctrinal, pastoral and spiritually warm, they could surpass the universities in theological education. There are not lacking examples from the past where this has been done, as in some of the dissenting academies of the eighteenth century and in the Free Church of Scotland colleges in the nineteenth. The opportunity is now here for the taking. Some of the denominational colleges are now stressing these points, as, for example, recent statements from Alister McGrath, the academically able Principal of Wycliffe Hall, Oxford, show.[18] Others seem frightened of departing from the university theology tradition. As a result, they cannot treat the message they are studying as Paul did when he said to the Thessalonians: 'You accepted it not as the word of men, but as it actually is, the word of God' (1 Thes. 2:13).

Theology in the rationalist tradition is really philosophy and not theology[19] because it depends on what the human mind can find acceptable. If evangelicals continue to teach theology in this tradition (even in evangelical colleges), they must expect to sterilize the preaching of many of their students, turn them into somewhat conservative liberals, and encourage an anti-theological attitude among lay people in the churches, which is growing in some circles. We cannot continue to teach theology through a rationalist methodology and expect to produce anything other than liberal evangelicals.

I believe that evangelicals must treat this issue with great seriousness if they are not to return to the situation of the 1930s, where ministerial trainees were so heavily infected by the rationalist tradition of university theology that they could no longer speak a word from God. If this happens again, CE leadership would be likely once more, in frustration at what they do not get from their official leadership, to pass to people with little doctrinal study behind them. That will make fanciful and unconvincing exposition too common and too acceptable. Already we find that lay people in the congregation can be better read and more doctrinally clued up than their theologically trained ministers, who seem to have studied everything except biblical doctrine and ethics. Since CEs claim to be Bible Christians, they must bring all the relevant resources of learning into the service of rightly understanding the Bible, not forgetting that without the enlightenment of the Holy Spirit they will never get it right. With that enlightenment they can hope to fulfil the awesome responsibility of bringing a message that is not just 'the present state of scholarly opinion' (which will change), or 'what I feel God has said to me', but an exposition of God's word.

8. LOOKING BACK, REACHING FORWARD

It seems clear that the evangelicals (particularly the CEs) of the 1930s were generally too anti-intellectual and too anti-theological. As a result, they were often superficial and their apologetics quite inadequate. They could be negative about secular 'high' culture because they did not know how to relate to the 'modern mind' of their day. They had, of course, a rich popular culture of their own, but they had become defensive and sometimes sharply contentious, though that was difficult to avoid when they were constantly under fire. To the exclusion of all else, they concentrated on the basics – sometimes called 'the simple gospel' – teaching the Bible and getting on with straightforward evangelism and missionary work, at which they were very good. That gave them plenty of scope, but they failed to recapture the theological training that they had left to others, and few of them who studied theology were uninfluenced by the prevailing liberalism. They had a splendid, if not very deeply doctrinal, knowledge of the Bible, and that gave great toughness to ordinary church members; but they lost many of their ablest young people and ministers in training to other traditions. For lack of a well-thought-out position they tended towards negative pietism and a legalistic stance in ethics – a short-cut solution to complex questions. In reaction to liberal 'social gospel' advocates they defended a negative attitude to social action, apart from immediate local philanthropy.

Mistaken reactions
In an attempt to break out of this too tight and too negative position, two different strategies started to be developed in the 1920s, and became

important in the 1930s and 1940s. One, represented by the Oxford Group/ Moral Rearmament, sought direct words from God ('guidance') apart from the Bible, and this gradually replaced the Bible in authority, both in personal 'quiet times' and in corporate strategy. It also led to a gradual loss of biblical and doctrinal content in the stress on experience and superficial 'life-changing' evangelism.

The other strategy, represented by the Anglican Evangelical Group Movement and the Fellowship of the Kingdom, was to borrow from the current culture, and that meant borrowing from a rationalist tradition. The message was progressively stripped of its offensive 'supernatural' elements until it became little different from the best humanistic outlook.

The Student Christian Movement, with its positive enthusiasms and its strong CE roots, had lost its way by trying to draw in leaders and speakers from all sections of the churches on to its platform. It spoke of wanting to stand in the current mainstream of theological tradition. In the prevailing theological scene, that meant that it also moved to a frankly liberal theological position as far as it could be said to have had one.

These movements may have had the best of motives, but they had the most disastrous of theologies. They experienced success for a time. To conservatives it seemed to be a kind of theological kwashiorkor – the deceptive result of a poor diet, or of deprivation of biblical food. Before long, however, they died of a lack of biblical input, while those who had a good diet gained strength, especially those who loved biblical doctrine and tried to base the Christian life upon it in the way that the New Testament does.

If we had lived then, we might well have made the same mistakes. It was a difficult time for the churches. They were losing ground, and it was easy to think that the old paths were no good. If we can learn from both the failures and the successes of the past, we may be helped to avoid falling into the same traps and to look for some guidelines for the future. No doubt there are new dangers also, but we need not repeat history.

The evangelical recovery

What, then, did establish evangelicals as a major feature of church life? By the 1930s a group of CEs was beginning to appear who had broken free from the rather defensive and negatively pietistic tradition, and in the 1940s and 1950s they were creating a new and vigorous CE cause. They were more doctrinally minded and therefore more confident and better equipped intellectually. There were older CE ministers in all four countries of the UK. Many of them now rallied round to support the infant IVF, and so reached an important slice of the new generation, including a growing number of future ministers. Martyn Lloyd-Jones, Daniel Lamont, some of the Free Church of Scotland professors and other strong individuals in all four countries, in associating themselves with the IVF, faced some increased unpopularity. But they provided the help that it needed to recapture ground in the world of thought, including academic theology, from the liberal consensus. Randle Manwaring[1] is not the only one to give a very negative picture of the outlook of the early members of the IVF regarding society, culture and intellectual effort. If it was true of many of the rank and file because that was their church tradition, it was not true of DJ and his circle, and most of the leaders and the speakers they chose. At a wartime IVF leaders' consultation, one of the only three field staff called on them 'to make history'.[2] It was no longer merely a holding operation. They were ready and better able than most to fight for the truth, and they fought well.

After the war, John Stott, William Still and a crowd of younger ministers and lay people emerged gradually to extend the frontiers of CE influence in all directions. Adrian Hastings (a Roman Catholic historian) describes John Stott as the most influential person in this period.[3] He may be right, but he does not note the previous and continuing influence of Lloyd-Jones, DJ and a considerable group of others who laboured before Stott became influential.

I believe that it is possible to identify four key factors in this recovery. First, it seems clear that one of the most important factors was that *they loved biblical doctrine*. In particular, they recovered a stronger and more biblical view of God. Others still shared their love of biblical ethics, but they were distinguished, both from their evangelical parents and from others in the churches, by a serious desire to re-establish biblical theology in the plain sense of that term and to fight to give it recognition. As John Stott put it in the 1950s, they wanted to work until their blood ran bibline! A relatively new kind of *doctrinal biblical preaching*, that had been rare, became common.[4] This shifted attention from the preacher to the Bible itself, and encouraged people to study it for themselves. It satisfied the hearers, who were not accepting the flights of fancy of some evangelical preachers, and it constantly exposed and taught the doctrines that were implicit, if not explicit, in the passage or topic under consideration.

Secondly, they wanted to find the *whole biblical outlook* that was derived from careful study of the text and focused in Jesus Christ. From a variety of different people there came together a fresh understanding of the unity of Christian truth, so that particular parts of it made more sense. This vision of the great biblical scheme from creation to eternity captured the evangelical community in a new way, and gave depth to both preaching and evangelism. This made it important to develop a more robust evangelical scholarship, as represented by the development of IVF literature and the setting up of Tyndale House and London Bible College, among other initiatives. They recovered more of the mainstream Reformation emphases when they worked at biblical teaching in greater depth. Those who have a good grasp of biblical doctrine cannot be anti-intellectual. Indeed, they should gain a fresh confidence in the superiority of its truth that leads them, like Paul, to aim to 'take captive every thought to make it obedient to Christ' (2 Cor. 10:5) and to believe that in principle that can be done. It is possible to argue whether anti-intellectualism is the parent or the child of an anti-theological attitude. What is clear, however, is that anti-intellectualism fails when there is a recovery of depth in biblical doctrines.

Thirdly, the recovery of belief in the almighty power, wisdom, sovereignty and awesome holiness of God helped evangelicals to be more confident, more thorough in their attempt to *love God with all their minds*, and to be willing to tackle any and every field of knowledge. The old defensiveness was lost. They believed that there are Christian approaches to be worked out in every sphere, from academic theology to art, science, education and medicine, and in society. Evangelism and apologetics were greatly improved. Many were, by God's special blessing, converted and then well taught.

Fourthly, the recovery of certain biblical themes *gave them the tools* to grapple with the world of culture, society and current thought generally. Among other things they recovered a belief in God's providential rule in nature and in history. They rediscovered a faith in God's generous (common grace) gifts even to fallen humanity, so that they did not dismiss all actions and artefacts of non-Christians as hopeless. They were therefore better able to appreciate what is good (by biblical criteria) in secular culture generally and in spheres such as art, literature and science, and to work with it. As Calvin had put it, they were able to 'look for honey even in the lion's mouth'. They began to have a doctrine of the state, and to see that one of the uses of God's law is to restrain evil in society; it is not only to bring people to Christ.[5] They had the ability to develop a more biblical doctrine of work, so that people in ordinary tasks could see their role as a vocation and give their minds to doing the job well. A belief that 'everything God created is good' (1 Tim. 4:4) enabled them to value the material world and to have an approach to the environment and to society. They recovered a responsibility to alter society for the better, which had been such a marked feature of the evangelicals of the early nineteenth century. In brief, they had arrived nearer to a biblically balanced position. They appeared to be more mature, even though their distinctive doctrines were (and are today) even more outrageous to the secular world than they had seemed in the 1930s.

From the end of the war, it was classical evangelicalism that resurrected the evangelical cause and led it for decades without rivals. It was not, however, just a revival of doctrine. It was a recovery of a living, preachable and preached doctrine. Many evangelical leaders were then, are today, and have typically always been, preachers. If in this study we have had to highlight people like Martyn Lloyd-Jones, John Stott, William Still and Billy Graham, and lay speakers and apologists such as Norman Anderson and Donald MacKay, they were only the most prominent. They provided helpful models. But a crowd of younger preachers, speakers and writers, many of whom had been recently converted, created the new evangelical cause. There was an explosion of biblical ministry that, by God's unusual blessing, swept away much of the dryness, defensiveness and superficiality or liberalism that had dominated the evangelicalism of the 1930s. With a foundation in a recovery of doctrinal depth, it was a spiritual renewal upon which the subsequent developments were built. This made possible the extension of evangelical influence and fitted CEs more adequately for responsibility in the churches and in society.

1995

What, then, of the present and the future? The portion of history I have sketched suggests strongly that evangelicalism will not advance by cultural and intellectual compromise, as advocated in the LE tradition. Nor will it advance by reliance on extrabiblical 'guidance', as in the Oxford Group/MRA. In the 1990s, we are faced with some of the same temptations as they were in the 1930s. It is again a very difficult time for the churches, and it is attractive to try to find some new theological emphases that resonate with the current culture. The danger is that, as many evangelicals did then, we should either compromise the truth or dilute it to a point where there is little biblical substance left. In a human-centred and experience-oriented generation that is earnestly seeking feel-good factors, it is not so easy to declare a word from God that is more than just the best and most attractive idea to our generation. When our hearers are human-centred, it is easy to follow them and to cease to be God-centred. As David Wells has put it: 'In these last three decades . . . Christian truth went from being an end in itself to being merely the means to personal healing.'[6] The soothing Thought for the Day on radio and the bland 'spirituality' of an outlook influenced by New Age sound more attractive. There is a danger of trying so hard to communicate with that culture in its own terms that we absorb too much of its influences, as the LEs did in the 1930s and 1940s.

If we, quite rightly, recognize some good in the culture and thinking of non-Christians and of other Christian traditions, then we need to be even better informed doctrinally if we are to discern the good from the evil and not to swallow them both together. The old clear-cut positions were in the short run easier to maintain in a simple way, but things are not all black and white and in the long run that position resulted in the loss of many of the more thinking young evangelicals. It is almost certain to do so again if there is not a good foundation in biblical teaching of considerable depth.

There is also a growing tendency to follow the policy that was so disastrous in the SCM of seeking to have 'important' people as platform speakers and, just because of their status, applauding their largely irrelevant pronouncements as if they were clear biblical thinkers. We are easily flattered by the attentions of those with big names, and the desire to be recognized or accepted contains a hidden trap that leads to pride. We must keep fighting for the truth, even if it gives offence.

At the same time, we are undoubtedly in danger in some circles of a renewed anti-intellectualism and anti-doctrinal superficiality that can feed on implausible uses of Bible verses out of context, especially when coupled with dogmatic statements about what is God's will. Our age is experience-centred, and as a result unstable in almost all relationships. We therefore do well to be aware of the instability, and of the inadequacy from a biblical point of view, of an experience-oriented religion such as was fostered by the Oxford Group/ MRA. If experience is stressed at the expense of doctrine (that is, truth) we are in trouble. Jesus was twice described in John 1 as 'full of grace *and* truth' (verse 14, *cf.* verse 17), and Peter urges us to 'grow in the grace *and* knowledge of our Lord and Saviour Jesus Christ' (2 Pet. 3:18). We dare not think that either a little grace or a little truth is sufficient. Therefore we must not run away from the theological and intellectual challenges of our time. We must develop a consistent evangelical theological training. Based upon a good foundation in biblical doctrine, evangelicals should be able to press ahead confidently into every area of thought and practice, and increasingly recapture ground that has been lost to serious Christian influence by liberalism and other distortions and dilutions of apostolic Christianity.

The greatest threat to evangelical strength, therefore, comes if we slip into superficiality of biblical input and fail to address the relative biblical illiteracy of our generation. If we do fail, we shall leave our hearers vulnerable to the latest errors, both at the top academic level and at the 'pop culture' or New Age level. We could again see something like the renewal of a vigorous LE movement on the one hand and a superficial and unstable experience-based pietism on the other. If the form of the disciplined early morning 'quiet time' has to change for many, some better way has to be found.

A good biblical diet may not seem as immediately exciting as a more experience-based approach. As with physical food, however, the attraction of unhealthy foods not only fails to make strong bodies but can produce a dependence on elements that put no iron into the blood or calcium into the bones. We need reserves for the tough days, and the Bible sometimes finds the solution to practical problems in the most surprising and apparently rather obscure corners of revealed truth. We see an example when Paul addresses the questions of going to law with fellow Christians and of immorality with his counter-question *'Do you not know . . .?'* (1 Cor. 6:3, 9, 19).

Ministers and youth leaders easily forget that the input that they provide – often only one service on Sunday – is far from being enough for those with little background of biblical knowledge. D. A. Carson puts it trenchantly: 'The ignorance of basic Scripture is so disturbing in our day that Christian preaching that does not seek to remedy the lack is simply irresponsible.'[7] Compared with the 1930s and even the 1940s and 1950s, evangelicals are now weak in the biblical content put into work with children and young people. Merely orthodox doctrine is no substitute for the Bible, which has unique spiritual power. That is not to suggest that merely having our heads stuffed with knowledge of the text of the Bible will in itself provide spiritual power. It is, however, a uniquely effective foundation for spiritual growth, and the Holy Spirit evidently inspired the Scriptures so that they should be his most reliable guide to spiritual life and maturity.

There are two main streams emerging in the evangelical community, and this division may prove more fundamental in its long-term effects than any other. It runs right across denominational distinctions, charismatic and non-charismatic divisions and any special-interest and party groupings. It is between those who make the Bible effectively, and not only theoretically, the mainstay of their ministry, and those who do not. Those who seek to clarify, teach and apply the Bible's message as their controlling principle and as the daily sustenance of the individual will, if this period of history is any

139

indication, produce strong Christians who are able to grapple with all kinds of issues in life, and to face the really tough experiences when they come. Those who fail to use the Bible in this way are almost certain to produce vulnerable Christians or painfully dependent people, who dare not move out from the particular congregation where they have been supported unless they can go somewhere else where they will be equally propped up. Exposure to a new cultural and intellectual atmosphere or a personal crisis will find them weak.

Experiences that chime in with the present culture may be good, or they may not. The Bible, however, as the Holy Spirit's chosen method of guiding the church throughout time, has outlived a thousand generations of different experiences and influences. As Peter reminds us, leaders, even church leaders, come and go 'like grass', while 'the word of the Lord stands for ever' (1 Pet. 1:24–25). A stress on experiences has too easily become human-centred. Unless our faith is truly centred on God and on what he has revealed of himself and 'his ways', we shall be swept off our feet by every latest fad of television culture and the chase for pious feel-good factors. That means that ministry today has to be willing to teach, and to make attractive, the great truths that are so carefully expounded in the more doctrinal parts of the gospels and letters, as well as in the Old Testament. Many failures are due to the lack of a proper doctrine of God.

John Stott, writing in 1990 on Paul's preaching to the Athenians, as recorded in Acts 17, comments: 'We learn from Paul that we cannot preach the gospel of Jesus without the doctrine of God, or the cross without the creation, or salvation without judgment.'[8]

One feature of the 1990s that is an enormous gain over the period of the 1930s is that there is a much larger core of biblically based and well-thought-out CE preaching and teaching, seeking to love God with all the heart, soul, strength and mind. Much of it has greater doctrinal depth than it had in the prewar period, and provides the main engine of evangelical church life. If we can resist the temptations to drift off to the right or the left, or to rest in the confidence of our relative success, classical evangelicalism should remain the backbone of evangelical life in the future. If we fail, on the one hand it could become unhelpfully academic or careless of biblical authority so as to tempt both liberalism and cultural compromise. On the other, it could become so weak in biblical content and in favour of a superficial 'spirituality' that it is driven by every 'wind of teaching' (Eph. 4:14) or immediately fashionable idea. The basic core is, however, stronger, more widespread and more understanding of the times than it has been for a long time. There are varieties of emphasis within it, and that is not unhealthy, so long as the appeal is always to the Bible as the final authority in faith and conduct and the Bible is really brought to bear on daily life. It was said of the early nineteenth-century evangelicals (such as Wilberforce and Shaftesbury) that they 'out-thought and out-lived' their contemporaries. Biblically informed Christians should be able to do so again.

What no-one can predict is whether there will be a strong enough core to build on the gains that have been made. It will be essential to keep the central truths central – 'to keep the fundamentals fundamental', as it has been repeatedly expressed. Only so will evangelical strength be maintained and increased, and an adequate base provided for grappling with the intellectual, social and personal problems of each new generation. It must also be said that, if we want to grow in influence, we must beware of self-congratulation and be marked by being a people who truly depend on God, as shown by our prayerfulness. As Psalm 127:1 warns us: 'Unless the LORD builds the house, its builders labour in vain.'

It is of doubtful value to seek evangelical unity as an end in itself, and recent efforts to do so have not succeeded greatly. Unity is important chiefly in so far as it creates a united *witness* to the great biblical revelation, so that the world can hear a clear message presented in a fitting way by both word and life when generally, in public, there is confusion as to what the message is. That requires basic agreement in doctrine. Evangelicalism is essentially distinguished from other Christian positions by a doctrinal stance derived from the Bible. We shall find unity not in our varied experiences but in the Word of God.

It is not at all original to point out that, when Joshua was commissioned to undertake the greatest reconquest in the history of Israel, he was not given a course in management, leadership, military strategy or other no doubt useful disciplines. He was, rather, told to meditate on the law day and night, and not to turn from obedience to it to the right or to the left, so that he might be successful wherever he went (Jos. 1). In the same way, Psalm 1, after describing the ungodly as those who walk in the counsel of the wicked, stand in the way of sinners and sit in the seat of mockers, describes the godly in terms of just one feature. They are those whose delight is in the law of the Lord so that they meditate on it day and night and whatever they do prospers. The New Testament is equally clear that the great secret of spiritual blessing and effectiveness is to be controlled by the revelation entrusted to the apostles and given to us in the Bible.

It is easy to be distracted from giving and accepting a good biblical diet by all sorts of relative side-issues. There are important lessons to be learned by the evangelical community from these sixty years. One of the most important is that we must improve the biblical input at both the simplest level and at the most sophisticated. This is the essential life-blood of all apostolic Christianity, and that is what genuine evangelicalism aspires to become.

All down the centuries God has blessed the recovery of biblical truth, and we cannot expect to find a greater blessing in anything else. There must be commitment to *biblical* Christianity in dependence on the Holy Spirit to enable us to understand the Bible, and to apply its teaching to ourselves and to the hearts and minds of believers and unbelievers alike. Given that foundation, it should be possible to recapture for a more nearly biblical position much more of the life and thought of the churches and, from there, of the life and thought of the community. It will not be easy, but we cannot aim for less. We must pray for that, and work in genuine dependence upon the God who alone is able to bring it about.

NOTES

1. WHO IS AN EVANGELICAL?

1 This is how John Stott's booklet *What is an Evangelical?* (Falcon, 1977) is often summarized, as, for example, by Clive Calver in *Together We Stand: Evangelical Convictions, Unity and Vision*, by Clive Calver and Rob Warner (Hodder and Stoughton, 1996), p. 26. It was a quick response by John Stott to a request for a definition.

2 *Make the Truth Known* (IVP, 1983), p. 3.

3 D. W. Bebbington, *Evangelicalism in Modern Britain: A History from the 1730s to the 1980s* (Unwin Hyman, 1989).

4 Alister E. McGrath, *A Passion for Truth: The Intellectual Coherence of Evangelicalism* (Apollos, 1996), p. 22.

5 Bebbington, *Evangelicalism*, p. 15.

6 See, for instance, Alan Acheson, *A True and Lively Faith: Evangelical Revival in the Church of Ireland* (Church of Ireland Evangelical Fellowship, 1992) and *History of the Church of Ireland 1691–1996* (APCK and Columba Press, 1977). Of the revived preachers, it was said that in contrast to others they 'preached Christ'.

7 McGrath, *A Passion for Truth*, p. 122.

8 See, for example, Calver and Warner, *Together We Stand*, chapter 2. This volume was published to celebrate 150 years of the Evangelical Alliance. Also see D. J. Tidball, *Who are the Evangelicals?* (Marshall Pickering, 1994).

9 D. W. Bebbington, 'Evangelicalism in Modern Scotland', *Scottish Bulletin of Evangelical Theology* 9 (1991).

10 The full title was The Inter-Varsity Fellowship of Evangelical Christian Unions (dropping the word 'Christian' soon after the start, as superfluous). The name was changed to the Universities and Colleges Christian Fellowship in 1975. Its publications were over the imprint 'Inter-Varsity Fellowship' until 1968, from when they appeared mostly over the imprint 'Inter-Varsity Press' or 'Tyndale Press'.

11 See the histories of the SCM/IVF/UCCF: Tissington Tatlow, *The Story of the Student Christian Movement of Great Britain and Ireland* (SCM, 1933), Douglas Johnson, *Contending for the Faith* (IVP, 1979) and Geraint Fielder, *Lord of the Years* (IVP, 1988).

12 The Doctrinal Basis was altered by the addition of two clauses in 1959; one on

the church, in response to criticisms that it was not even mentioned, and the other a clause on the sovereignty of God in response to the growing awareness of a gap. The order of the clauses was also changed to start with a clause about God, rather than the one about the Bible. See the details in the histories listed in n. 11 above. Putting God first represented a recognition that that is where theology should begin, and a move from a more defensive response to liberalism that had dominated the 1930s.

2. PREWAR DOLDRUMS

1 This was a lecture given by a member of the theology faculty in Cambridge, on 'The Decline of the Evangelical Party in the Nineteenth Century' (I am almost certain that it was Charles Smyth). Professor Adrian Hastings agrees with the first point. He wrote that the evangelical weakness was 'to some extent the consequence of the preponderant missionary concern of the late nineteenth-century evangelicals. It had creamed off their best men overseas for several decades, leaving little that was exciting to lead evangelical ranks at home.' A. Hastings, *A History of English Christianity, 1920–1985* (Collins, 1986), p. 76. On the second point, the lecturer I heard spoke of spending their energies in 'putting innocent high-churchmen like myself in prison'.

2 From correspondence with the Rev. William J. Johnston, Rector of Killskerry, who is researching the period.

3 This may seem too sweeping in view of the relatively orthodox position of some, and the influence of the 'biblical theology movement' led by Edwyn Hoskyns and then C. H. Dodd; but even the more orthodox had a firmly liberal stance in relation to the reliability of the Bible.

4 From an unpublished autobiographical memorandum by the late Rev. John Wenham.

5 Sir William Joynson-Hicks was Home Secretary from 1924 to 1929; Sir Thomas Inskip was Solicitor-General and, as Lord Caldecote, became Lord Chancellor in 1939. Henson was incensed at the way in which these two had led the defeat of the 1928 Prayer Book in the House of Commons.

6 Stephen Neill, *Anglicanism* (Pelican, 1958), p. 400, quoted in Randle Manwaring, *From Controversy to Co-existence: Evangelicals in the Church of England, 1914–1980* (Cambridge University Press, 1985).

7 W. O. E. Oesterley and Theodore H. Robinson, *Hebrew Religion: Its Origin and Development* (SPCK, 1930, 2nd edn 1937), pp. 45, 28. It was constantly reprinted.

8 Ronald Knox, *Essays in Satire* (Sheed and Ward, 1928).

9 Some strong CEs did survive in Spurgeon's College to have a big influence later, as did people like John Wenham in other places, but their number was not large.

10 Oak Hill and Clifton were started in 1932, Oak Hill being based on Bohun Lodge, which prepared those without School Certificate for that exam before going on to ministerial training. In the 1930s Oak Hill averaged twenty-five students, of whom a number were doing School Certificate first. The BCMS College in Bristol was partly to train missionaries in short courses of Bible knowledge.

11 Ieuan Phillips became Superintendent of the Forward Movement of the Presbyterian Church of Wales. Roland Lamb became an IVF travelling secretary after

the war, a minister in Aberystwyth, and finally Secretary of the British Evangelical Council.

12 T. C. Hammond was Superintendent of the Irish Church Missions and left to become the Principal of Moore Theological College, Sydney. See his biography by Warren Nelson, *T. C. Hammond: His Life and Legacy in Ireland and Australia* (Banner of Truth, 1994). Daniel Lamont was Professor of Apologetics at Edinburgh from 1927 to 1939, and from 1939 to 1945 he held the new Chair of Christian Ethics and Practical Theology, into which the other professorship had been merged.

13 See C. Armitage, *Reaching for the Goal: The Life Story of David Adeney* (Harold Shaw, 1993).

14 Lord Robbins, *Report on Higher Education* (HMSO, 1963), gives 1.7% actually in universities, 0.7% in teacher training colleges and 0.3% in further education (mostly in technical colleges).

15 See n. 4 above.

16 C. E. Raven, *The Wanderer's Way* (1928).

17 It is important to distinguish 'rationalism' – the view that reason is the final source of all wisdom and authority – from the need to be rational in our attempts to digest and understand all the data that God may give us in revelation and in nature. The first amounts to asserting that 'I will believe only what seems reasonable to me'; the second sees human reason as one of the tools that God has given us to understand the data. The scientist's desire to 'sit down before the facts' and try to understand them, however strange they may be, is quite different from making 'what I think is reasonable' the criterion of which facts I will accept. The attitude of 'sitting down before the facts' comes near to the attitude of evangelicals to the

biblical revelation, which is perhaps one reason why evangelicals have often been prominent in science.

18 The Irish and Welsh Prayer Books had been modified in some respects.

19 Jack Watford, *Yesterday and Today: A History of Crusaders* (Crusaders' Union, 1995), and Helen Roseveare, *On Track: The Story of The Girl Crusaders' Union* (Girl Crusaders' Union, 1990). In Leicester alone there were 443 boys on the class lists in 1937 (513 in 1961), and four girls' classes in 1961 with 178 on the roll. An analysis of the church connections of the leaders shows that they came from a good variety of denominations (correspondence with Colin Densham, who was one of the leaders and has written records). Crusaders were also strong in some parts of Scotland.

20 Frederick P. Wood and Mary S. Wood, *Youth Advancing: The Story of what God has Done through the National Young Life Campaign, 1911–1961* (NYLC, no date).

21 See Brynmor Jones, *King's Champions, 1863–1933* (privately published, 1968) and Geraint D. Fielder, *Excuse Me, Mr Davies – Hallelujah! Evangelical Student Witness in Wales, 1923–1983* (Evangelical Press of Wales and IVP, 1983).

22 Geraint Fielder has supplied a number of these points in correspondence. He quoted from the magazine *Efengylydd* in 1925: 'the Lord has thousands of saints in every denomination. If he is not going to rapture them, He may well separate them to be a Church unto Himself.'

23 See the massive biography by Iain H. Murray, *D. Martyn Lloyd-Jones*, vol. 1: *The First Forty Years, 1899–1939*; vol. 2: *The Fight of Faith, 1939–1981* (Banner of Truth, 1982, 1990).

24 Many Brethren assemblies have by the 1990s adopted the title 'Evangelical

Church', and so are not seen as in the Brethren tradition, though in fact they retain many of its emphases.

25 There is a handwritten autobiographical sketch giving some details of his life.

26 See John Eddison (ed.), *A Study of Spiritual Power: An Appreciation of E. J. H. Nash* (rev. edn Highland, 1992).

27 F. D. Coggan (ed.), *Christ and the Colleges: A History of the IVFEU* (IVF, 1934). Coggan, later to become Archbishop of Canterbury, was at that time editor of the IVF's magazine *Inter-Varsity*.

28 Manwaring, *From Controversy to Co-existence*, p. 45.

29 Daniel Lamont, *Christ and the World of Thought* (T. and T. Clark, 1934).

30 The conference addresses were published under the title *Christ our Freedom* (IVF, 1939). The preacher at the communion service was the Rev. W. H. Aldis (an Anglican), the Chairman of Keswick and Home Director of the China Inland Mission.

31 Owen Chadwick, *Michael Ramsey* (Clarendon, 1990). Ramsey (1904–1988) was Archbishop of Canterbury from 1961 to 1974. See also a full account of the mission in J. C. Pollock's history of the CICCU, *A Cambridge Movement* (John Murray, 1953).

32 T. C. Hammond, *In Understanding be Men* (IVF, 1936; revised by David F. Wright, IVP, 1968).

33 Letter from Miss Muriel Crouch FRCS, who became a consultant surgeon and a valued speaker, especially among medical students, after the war.

34 The detailed list is in Coggan, *Christ and the Colleges*, and the histories of the Crusaders' Unions cited in n. 19 above.

35 There are analogies with the 1970s and 1980s, and in calling some of these initiatives 'renewal movements' I want

to draw out some of the similarities with movements that later adopted that title. Renewal was what they hoped to achieve.

36 I am indebted to Ian Randall's paper, 'Life-Changing: The Oxford Group as a Movement of Spiritual Renewal', *Christianity and History Newsletter* 16 (1996), and to correspondence with him, as well as to personal memories and other books by Oxford Group leaders.

37 Randall, 'Life-Changing'.

38 David Adeney. See Armitage, *Reaching for the Goal*, p. 36.

39 I am indebted to an unpublished paper by Dr Martin Davie and conversation and correspondence with him, and to his *British Quaker Theology Since 1895* (Edwin Mellen, 1997). A decisive emergence of 'a new liberal Quakerism' is seen in the Manchester Conference of 1895.

40 Randall, 'Life-Changing'.

41 I am indebted to Ian Randall, *Quest, Crusade and Fellowship: The Spiritual Formation of the Fellowship of the Kingdom* (Fellowship of the Kingdom, 1995).

42 See Ian Randall, 'Southport and Swanwick: Contrasting Movements of Methodist Spirituality in Inter-war England', *Proceedings of the Wesley Historical Society* 50 (1995).

43 See V. F. Storr (ed.), *Liberal Evangelicalism: An Interpretation* (1923) and *Freedom and Tradition: A Study of Liberal Evangelicalism* (1940). There is also a very useful paper by Ian Randall, 'The Evangelical Group Movement in the Church of England', *Anglican and Episcopal History* 65.3 (1996).

44 Randall, 'Evangelical Group Movement', quoting an article by Edward Woods. See also Oliver Tomkins, *The Life of Edward Woods* (SCM, 1957). Woods was at the time Bishop of

Croydon and later of Lichfield. While he was a student he had been a zealous CE. He had moved his position when he served on the staff of Ridley Hall, Cambridge, in 1904–6.

45 Tomkins, *The Life of Edward Woods.*

46 Raven's best work is regarded as his study of the seventeenth-century scientist John Ray, but he also wrote on science and religion in *Natural Religion and Christian Theology* (Cambridge University Press, 1953) and other works.

47 Letter from Chavasse's personal chaplain, Rev. R. J. B. Eddison, to whom the bishop related the incident.

48 J. R. S. Taylor is sometimes confused with Bishop J. Taylor-Smith, who had been Chaplain-General to the Forces during World War 1 and in his retirement was a popular speaker at IVF conferences and other CE meetings.

49 It was those who had been students in the 1930s who, as bishops, moderators, professors and so on in the 1950s and 1960s, attacked Billy Graham and CEs generally.

50 See Tissington Tatlow, *The Story of the Student Christian Movement of Great Britain and Ireland* (SCM, 1933).

51 See, for example, M. Saward and P. Barron in C. Yeats (ed.), *Has Keele Failed?* (Hodder and Stoughton, 1995).

52 Manwaring, *From Controversy to Co-existence.*

3. THE CRUCIBLE OF WAR: 1939–45

1 Lord Rochester had been a Liberal MP and was Paymaster-General in the House of Lords from 1931 to 1936, representing the Ministry of Labour there in Ramsay Macdonald's government during the Depression. See *The Times* obituary, 14 January 1955.

2 A. J. Vereker, a layman and nephew of Lord Gort, was secretary of the Crusaders

Union (*i.e.* Boys') from 1919 to 1946.

3 After five years as a missionary in China with the China Inland Mission, the Rev. A. M. Stibbs returned and joined the staff of Oak Hill College in 1937, becoming Vice-Principal in 1940 and remaining on the staff there until shortly before his death in 1971.

4 These were the IVF, the Crusaders' Union, the Girl Crusaders' Union and the Children's Special Service Mission, which changed its name to Scripture Union in 1959.

5 Present were A. W. Churchill (a publisher) in the chair, Brian Aldis (then chairman of the IVF student Executive Committee and an Anglican ordinand), Montague Goodman (Brethren), the Rev. H. R. Gough (Anglican), John Laing (Brethren), the Rev. J. Chalmers Lyon (English Presbyterian), and the Rev. J. Pritchard, with A. J. Vereker and DJ.

6 Details in T. A. Noble, *A Brief History of Tyndale House and the Tyndale Fellowship* (forthcoming). In all, fifteen people were present.

7 Lloyd-Jones's 1952–55 Friday evening lectures illustrate this well: see *Great Doctrines*, vol. 1: *God the Father, God the Son* (Hodder and Stoughton, 1996). The quotations are from pp. 34, 245–246 and 94 respectively.

8 The earlier preaching of Lloyd-Jones exemplifies this best, and gives some idea of its impact. See his *The Life of Joy: Studies in Philippians 1 and 2* and *The Life of Peace: Studies in Philippians 3 and 4* (Hodder and Stoughton, 1993, but preached in 1947–8); *Expository Sermons on 2 Peter* (Banner of Truth, 1983, preached in 1946–7); and his sermons on Habakkuk (*From Fear to Faith*) and Psalm 73 (*Faith on Trial*), republished together under the title *Faith Tried and Triumphant* (IVP, 1987, but preached in

the 1940s).

9 See Helen Roseveare's autobiographical studies *Give Me this Mountain* and *He Gave Us a Valley* (IVP, 1966, 1976, both reissued 1995), and David Hawker's biography of Ruth Watson, *Kanchi Doctor: Ruth Watson of Nepal* (Scripture Union, 1984).

10 See Geraint D. Fielder, *'Excuse Me, Mr Davies – Hallelujah!' Evangelical Student Witness in Wales, 1923–1983* (Evangelical Press of Wales and IVP, 1983).

11 They were eventually collected into one volume, the famous *Mere Christianity* (1952).

12 T. F. Torrance was Professor of Church History from 1950 to 1952 and of Church Dogmatics from 1952 to 1979. By the 1990s, other evangelicals in the Church of Scotland were working more closely with him to resist the growing liberal tendencies.

13 Quoted from a published letter of John Stott's in Martyn Eden and David F. Wells (eds.), *The Gospel in the Modern World: A Tribute to John Stott* (IVP, 1991), p. 23.

14 Correspondence and conversation with Sir Eric Richardson. I was also present at the meeting where it was decided to set up a separate technical colleges work. The work in the teacher training colleges was known as the Training Colleges Christian Union (TCCU), and that in the technical and art colleges as the Technical Colleges Christian Fellowship (TCCF). They held their own substantial conferences, but were firmly part of the IVF, contrary to the impression given in some writings. The distinct identity of TCCU and TCCF gave a great stimulus to students in these colleges to reach out to other similar colleges which could easily have been submerged in the larger university work. It also made possible a

concentration on their special needs and opportunities, which were in many ways distinct from those of the universities.

4. NEW BEGINNINGS: 1945–55

1 Opinion Research Centre, *Religion in Northern Ireland* (Independent Television Authority, Belfast, 1969).

2 See J. T. Carson (ed.) *Mission Completed: T. S. Mooney of Londonderry, 1907–86* (TSM Books, 1986). It is there reported that although in later life he 'recognised the need for radical change and constructive dialogue with the Roman Catholic Church and its people', he was for most of his life 'blinded by a comfortable pietism into the urgency of social issues'.

3 See G. D. Fielder, *'Excuse Me, Mr Davies – Hallelujah!' Evangelical Student Witness in Wales, 1923–1983* (Evangelical Press of Wales and IVP, 1983).

4 Personal memories of G. D. Fielder.

5 *Towards the Conversion of England* (Press and Publications Board of the Church Assembly, 1945).

6 In one Church of England college it was a parody of the communion service.

7 Personal conversation.

8 He was subsequently a university lecturer and leader in student work in Singapore and Malaysia.

9 *Basic Christianity* (IVP, 1958), revised in 1971 and repeatedly reprinted.

10 MacKay's most influential Christian books were probably *The Clockwork Image* (IVP, 1974, reissued 1996) and before that *Christianity in a Mechanistic Universe*, of which he was editor and key contributor (IVP, 1965). Other writings are posthumously collected in M. Tinker (ed.), *The Open Mind and Other Essays* (IVP, 1988).

11 This was Harold St John, in a personal conversation. He overstated the case, but it shows how far the IVF was seen by

some as the standard-bearer for the CE cause at that stage.

12 In response to criticisms, the IVF Basis had two clauses added later. See ch. 1, n. 12.

13 Fielder, *'Excuse Me, Mr Davies – Hallelujah!'*

14 See Nigel Sylvester, *God's Word in a Young World: The Story of Scripture Union* (Scripture Union, 1984).

15 See Sybil Dobbie, *Faith and Fortitude: The Life and Work of General Sir William Dobbie* (privately published, 1979).

16 D. W. Bebbington, *Evangelicalism in Modern Britain: A History from the 1730s to the 1980s* (Unwin Hyman, 1989), p. 259.

17 D. W. Bebbington, 'Evangelicalism in Modern Scotland', *Scottish Bulletin of Evangelical Theology* 9 (1991).

18 Ian M. Randall, 'Conservative Constructionist: The Early Influence of Billy Graham in Britain', *Evangelical Quarterly* 67.4 (1995), pp. 309–333; quotation from p. 332.

19 See Iain H. Murray, *D. Martyn Lloyd-Jones*, vol. 2: *The Fight of Faith, 1939–1981* (Banner of Truth, 1990).

20 R. V. G. Tasker, *The Narrow Way* (IVF, 1952). Previously he had published with the SCM.

21 *The Biblical Doctrine of the Wrath of God* (Tyndale Press, 1951).

22 Quoted in G. R. Balleine and Colliss Davies, *A Popular History of the Church of England* (Vine Books, 1976), p. 198.

23 Murray, *D. Martyn Lloyd-Jones*, vol. 2, gives details; pp. 228–229.

24 A. T. de B. Wilmot. See obituary in *Evangelicals Now*, February 1997.

25 Gottfried Osei-Mensah became Secretary of the Lausanne Committee, which followed the Lausanne Congress of 1974.

26 See Pete Lowman, *The Day of his Power: A History of the International Fellowship of Evangelical Students* (IVP, 1983).

27 Bebbington, *Evangelicalism in Modern Britain*, p. 250.

5. CONSOLIDATION: 1955–70

1 *Fundamentalism: A Religious Problem* (Times Publishing Co., 1955).

2 *The Bishoprick*, February 1956. Other features of this debate, and fuller quotations from the article in question, are given in O. R. Barclay, *Whatever Happened to the Jesus Lane Lot?* (IVP, 1977).

3 Gabriel Hebert, *Fundamentalism and the Church of God* (SCM, 1957).

4 J. I. Packer, *'Fundamentalism' and the Word of God* (IVF, 1958, reissued IVP, 1996).

5 Letter from Michael Griffiths. He was refused ordination on the grounds of his lack of enthusiasm for the baptism of children of non-churchgoers. He later became General Director of the OMF and then Principal of London Bible College.

6 Details are in Iain H. Murray, *D. Martyn Lloyd-Jones*, vol. 2: *The Fight of Faith, 1939–1981* (Banner of Truth, 1990).

7 J. I. Packer (ed.), *All in Each Place: Towards Reunion in England* (Marcham, 1965).

8 Discussed in some detail in Murray, *D. Martyn Lloyd-Jones*, vol. 2.

9 The entire statement under the heading 'Our Fellow Evangelicals' (item 93) reads: 'We value our present fellowship and co-operation with our fellow evangelicals in other Churches, to whom we are specially bound by a common understanding of the faith, and we desire a strengthening of these relations.' The entire Keele Statement is reprinted in C. Yeats (ed.), *Has Keele Failed?* (Hodder and Stoughton, 1995), where it occupies thirty-four pages, so clause 93 is hardly a major feature. J. Capon, *Evangelicals*

Tomorrow (Collins, 1977), which is a popular report of the subsequent Nottingham Congress held in 1977, has a good survey of how little this clause in the Keele Statement really meant in practice.

10 A complete bibliography of John Stott's writings up to 1994 occupies nearly 100 pages. See T. Dudley-Smith, *John Stott: A Comprehensive Bibliography* (IVP, 1995).

11 J. R. W. Stott, *Christ the Controversialist: A Study in Some Essentials of Evangelical Religion* (Tyndale Press, 1970, reissued IVP, 1996).

12 *Church of England Newspaper*, 16 March 1962.

13 This is exemplified as late as 1985 in a report of the British Council of Churches Evangelism Committee published in 1988, headed 'Visit of the Focus Group to Ireland'.

14 By 1995, the growth of CE churches outside the Church of England, and the lack of much effective influence of evangelicals within it, in spite of increased numbers and a sizeable group of bishops, began to make some Anglicans doubt whether this move to give greater priority to denominationalism was altogether a wise one (see pp. 119–121). Apart from the founders and supporters of Latimer House, it is not clear that many asked how to be more fully involved and still keep the clarity of their biblical witness at the grass roots. While the Eclectics had grown to over a thousand members and was committed to the final authority of Scripture, its interests were more pastoral than doctrinal.

15 Guthrie's *Introduction* actually appeared from the IVF in sections: *The Pauline Letters* (1961), *Hebrews to Revelation* (1962) and *The Gospels and Acts* (1965). It was first published by IVP in one volume (revised) in 1970 as *Introduction to the New Testament*.

16 Published by IVP in 1968 (reissued IVP, 1995). Schaeffer's rather larger book, published later in the same year, was *The God who is There* (Hodder and Stoughton). The manuscript for that had been ready first, but was held back by the publisher for fear that it would not sell, until the success of the IVP book assured it.

17 J. I. Packer, *Evangelism and the Sovereignty of God* (IVF, 1961).

18 *Pollution and the Death of Man* (Hodder and Stoughton, 1970).

19 Both published by IVF/IVP.

20 Hans Rookmaaker, *Modern Art and the Death of a Culture* (IVP, 1970, reprinted 1995).

21 See David Porter, *Arts and Minds: The Story of Nigel Goodwin* (Hodder and Stoughton, 1993).

22 *Ibid.*

23 All published by IVP, in 1967, 1968 and 1972 respectively.

24 See Timothy Chester, *Awakening to a World of Need: The Recovery of Evangelical Social Concern* (IVP, 1993).

25 *Into the World: The Need and Limits of Christian Involvement* (Falcon, 1968).

26 'A. N. Triton' was a pseudonym used by me while a senior staff member of the IVF so as to avoid any impression that what I wrote might be official policy – at least when it appeared controversial to some members.

27 H. F. R. Catherwood, *The Christian Citizen* (Hodder and Stoughton, 1969).

28 H. F. R. Catherwood, *The Christian in Industrial Society* (IVP, 1964), p. 14.

29 See Chester, *Awakening to a World of Need*, for a history.

30 By 1995 TEAR Fund's income was in the order of £23 million, far outstripping any British missionary society.

31 A. Hastings, *A History of English Christianity, 1920–1985* (Collins, 1986), p. 584.

32 Hastings, *History*, p. 552.

33 *The Making of a Counter-Culture* (Faber and Faber, 1970).

34 David F. Wells, *No Place for Truth, or Whatever Happened to Evangelical Theology?* (IVP, 1993), p. 210.

35 Hastings, *History*, p. 552.

36 J. A. T. Robinson, *Honest to God* (SCM, 1963).

37 *Idem, Christian Morals Today* (SCM, 1964). See also his *Christian Freedom in a Permissive Society* (SCM, 1970).

38 *Situation Ethics: The New Morality* (SCM, 1966).

39 Hastings, *History*, p. 554.

6. MORE ADVENTURE, LESS UNITY: 1970–80

1 Maurice A. P. Wood was made Bishop of Norwich. He was a former 'Bash Camper' and was regarded by many as the only CE bishop.

2 See Sir Norman Anderson, *An Adopted Son: The Story of My Life* (IVP, 1985).

3 Nigel Wright in *Evangelicals Now*, July 1995.

4 *Growing Into Union: Proposals for Forming a United Church in England* (SPCK, 1970). The four authors were Colin O. Buchanan, E. L. Mascall, J. I. Packer and G. D. Leonard.

5 *Obeying Christ in a Changing World*, 3 vols. (Collins, 1977). General Editor, John Stott. Quotations are from vol. 2: *The People of God*, ed. Ian Cundy, in the essay by him, p. 26.

6 D. N. Samuel (ed.), *The Evangelical Succession* (James Clarke, 1979), p. 108. Quoted in Randle Manwaring, *From Controversy to Co-existence: Evangelicals in the Church of England, 1914–1980* (Cambridge University Press, 1985).

7 See Douglas McBain, *Fire over the Waters: Renewal among Baptists from the 1960s to the 1990s* (Darton, Longman and Todd, 1997). The history of Mainstream is covered here, especially pp. 82–85.

8 Letter from Douglas McBain.

9 Details from Peter Brierley, *Christian England: What the English Church Census Reveals* (MARC Europe, 1991).

10 D. W. Bebbington, *Evangelicalism in Modern Britain: A History from the 1730s to the 1980s* (Unwin Hyman, 1989), p. 269.

11 There is a good discussion of the hermeneutical issues by J. I. Packer in M. Tinker (ed.), *Restoring the Vision: Anglican Evangelicals Speak Out* (Monarch, 1990).

12 Bebbington, *Evangelicalism in Modern Britain*.

13 Edited by John Hick (SCM, 1977).

14 Published by SCM in 1980.

15 Published by Falcon; revised edition by Kingsway in 1986. As an example of conference papers, see those from the National Evangelical Conference on Social Ethics under the title *Essays in Evangelical Social Ethics*, ed. D. F. Wright (Paternoster, 1979).

16 *Built as a City: God and the Urban World Today* (Hodder and Stoughton, 1974).

17 See, for instance, the violent criticism that Lord Shaftesbury received when he compromised over the Ten Hours Act in order to get some limitation of working hours on the statute book, rather than nothing. G. Battiscombe, *Shaftesbury: A Biography of the Seventh Earl, 1801–1885* (Constable, 1974).

18 Murray's book (Banner of Truth) explores the postmillennial position. Hendriksen's argued for an amillennial position. When it was published by the IVF in 1962 (USA edition, Baker, 1939), it aroused some controversy,

especially among the Brethren, most of whom were fairly strongly premillennial and were not pleased with the IVF for publishing it in the UK.

19 See, for instance, Gillian Wagner, *Barnardo* (Weidenfeld and Nicolson, 1979). Wagner sees the policies of Barnardo as very much those that formed the basis of our social services. See also Kathleen Heasman, *Evangelicals in Action: An Appraisal of their Social Work* (Geoffrey Bles, 1962), where the same point is elaborated.

20 Published by the InterVarsity Christian Fellowship in the USA and by Hodder and Stoughton in the UK.

21 R. J. Sider, with a Response by J. R. W. Stott, *Evangelism, Salvation and Social Justice* (Grove Books, 1977).

22 *Walk in his Shoes* (IVP, 1975), published in the USA under the title *Who is my Neighbor?* (IVP, 1976).

23 The Keele Covenant is given in full as Appendix A in C. Yeats (ed.), *Has Keele Failed?* (Hodder and Stoughton, 1995).

24 John Stott, *Explaining the Lausanne Covenant* (Scripture Union, 1975). The entire paragraph 5 is quoted in Timothy Chester, *Awakening to a World of Need: The Recovery of Evangelical Social Concern* (IVP, 1993), p. 69.

25 'Evangelical Social and Political Ethics: An Historical Perspective', *Evangelical Quarterly* 62.1 (1990), pp. 19–26.

26 *At the Cutting Edge* (Hodder and Stoughton, 1995).

27 See the biographies of the members of the Clapham Sect, such as William Wilberforce and Henry Thornton, *e.g.* Standish Meacham, *Henry Thornton of Clapham, 1760–1815* (Harvard University Press, 1964), and Charles Buxton, *Memoirs of Sir Thomas Fowell Buxton* (John Murray, 1849). The last two biographies have the advantage of extensive quotations from their private diaries to show their motives. Buxton saw the liberation of all slaves in the British dominions through Parliament in 1833, when Wilberforce was too ill to do it, after his long battle for the abolition of the slave trade (which had been successful in 1807).

7. ADJUSTING TO A CHANGING SOCIETY: 1980–95

1 Survey carried out by the Bible Society and the Evangelical Alliance of Wales: Geoffrey Fewkes, *Challenge to Change* (Bible Society, 1997). It is reported in the *Church of England Newspaper* of 12 April 1996 that its chairman says: 'Despite the decline, which we've all been aware of, it is delightful to see those churches with a strong Bible focus and a spirituality based on the daily use of Scripture are growing.'

2 In *Evangelicals Now*, December 1995.

3 Rodney Howard-Brown as reported in *Evangelicals Now*, February 1996.

4 Dave Tomlinson, *The Post-Evangelical* (SPCK, 1995). Tomlinson was formerly a leader in one of the 'new churches', but now appears so doctrinally loose that he does not have a clear position on a whole range of doctrines.

5 Nigel Wright, *The Radical Evangelical* (SPCK, 1996). Wright has written several pieces as a spokesperson for the charismatic wing of the churches, notably in Tom Smail, Andrew Walker and Nigel Wright, *Charismatic Renewal: The Search for a Theology* (SPCK, 1995). In his 1996 book he has moved to a less than CE position on several issues. He holds that the Bible is sometimes in error, that Jesus made 'innocent mistakes' and that substitutionary atonement is in some ways a misleading idea. It is relevant to remember his own warning given earlier (see p. 100).

6 It is often necessary to distinguish between what is right or wrong 'in the circumstances' and what is in an absolute sense good or evil. Lying is a destructive and evil thing, but it is possible to envisage situations where it is the lesser evil and therefore 'right in the circumstances'. This does nothing to undermine the claim that there are moral absolutes. See discussion in B. Kaye and G. Wenham (eds.), *Law, Morality and the Bible* (IVP, 1978).

7 *E.g.* Gavin J. McGrath, *A Confident Life in an Age of Change* (IVP, 1995), Alister McGrath, *A Passion for Truth: The Intellectual Coherence of Evangelicalism* (Apollos, 1996), and D. A. Carson, *The Gagging of God: Christianity Confronts Pluralism* (Apollos, 1996).

8 British Council of Churches Evangelism Committee report, 'Visit of the Focus Group to Ireland', 1–4 November 1985, published 1988.

9 Clive Calver and Rob Warner, *Together we Stand: Evangelical Convictions, Unity and Vision* (Hodder and Stoughton, 1996).

10 C. Yeats (ed.), *Has Keele Failed?* (Hodder and Stoughton, 1995).

11 *Issues Facing Christians Today* (Marshall, Morgan and Scott, 1984).

12 By 1996 Professor D. J. Wiseman had been active in the work of Tyndale House for fifty years (for thirty as its chairman) and is a major contributor to its work for publication.

13 Murray Harris, *Easter in Durham* (Paternoster, 1985).

14 See above, ch. 2 n. 17.

15 Historical theology can also be handled in such a way as to make it a very relativistic field.

16 See Bruce's *Paul, Apostle of the Free Spirit* (Paternoster, 1981).

17 Lloyd-Jones's address at the opening of the college is published under the title *Training for the Ministry Today* (London Theological Seminary, 1977).

18 McGrath, *A Passion for Truth*, pp. 15–22. 'Academic theologians occasionally refer to evangelicalism as "naïve" . . . this generally turns out to mean something like "refusing to acknowledge the *imperium* of the academy" . . . it focuses on the refusal of evangelicalism to become subservient to the ideology of what is coming to be seen as an increasingly marginalized and anti-religious academy' (p. 17).

19 DJ explored this point in one of his long memoranda for staff. Most modern academic theology is also still in the older 'modernist' tradition, where scientific knowledge is thought to be the ideal. It is therefore quite logical that in some universities the theology department has been assimilated into the philosophy department, and comparative 'religious studies' replaces Christian theology.

8. Looking back, reaching forward

1 See chapter 2, p. 28 and note 28.

2 This was Gordon Harman, an Anglican parson.

3 A. Hastings, *A History of English Christianity, 1920–1985* (Collins, 1986), pp. 455, 615–617.

4 The Reformers and then the influential Charles Simeon (1759–1836), and many others, had of course taught and set an example in expository preaching that kept closely to the original intention of the authors of the Bible. Simeon has been described as 'the father of expository preaching', but by the 1920s and 1930s that tradition was largely lost.

5 The Reformers frequently spoke of the threefold use of the law: to bring people to an awareness of sin, and so to Christ;

to guide the Christian's conduct (as in Eph. 4:26 – 6:3) and to restrain evil in society as expressed in 1 Tim. 1:8–11. This 'third use of the law' had often been forgotten. See, for instance, the Formula of Concord and other Reformation documents that explore it.

6 David F. Wells, *No Place for Truth, or Whatever Happened to Evangelical Theology?* (IVP, 1993), p. 210.

7 D. A. Carson, *The Gagging of God: Christianity Confronts Pluralism* (Apollos, 1996), p. 194.

8 J. R. W. Stott, *The Message of Acts* (IVP, 1990), p. 290.

INDEX

A Passion For Truth
The intellectual coherence of evangelicalism
ALISTER E. McGRATH

A passion for truth *considers the intellectual coherence of evangelicalism in terms of its likely future in a postmodern world, a world with competing ideologies and widely diverging theories of legitimization. A serious weakness has been the failure of evangelicalism to foster a contemporary Christian mind. This book sets out the basic groundwork and agenda for seriously attempting such a task. In so doing, it teases out the distinctiveness of evangelicalism against the backdrop of its current rivals – postliberalism, postmodernism and religious pluralism – but also reaffirms its living and particular foundation in Christ alone, as attested by Scripture.*

Evangelicalism, the author concludes, should feel confident about mounting a sustained bid for a justified presence within the academic community. It unashamedly remains a serious option for thinking men and women in today's world.

Alister McGrath is principal of Wycliffe Hall, Oxford, university research lecturer in theology at Oxford University, and research professor of systematic theology at Regent College, Vancouver.

287 pages   *Large Paperback*

APOLLOS